Stuart Yarr

Upgrading and Fixing a PC

to make your computer faster, more
versatile, and more powerful

In easy steps is an imprint of In Easy Steps Limited
Southfield Road · Southam
Warwickshire CV47 0FB · United Kingdom
www.ineasysteps.com

Second edition

Notice of Liability
Every effort has been made to ensure that this book contains accurate
and current information. However, In Easy Steps Limited and the
author shall not be liable for any loss or damage suffered by readers
as a result of any information contained herein.

Trademarks
Microsoft® and Windows® are registered trademarks of Microsoft
Corporation. All other trademarks are acknowledged as belonging to
their respective companies.

Printed and bound in the United Kingdom

ISBN-13 978-1-84078-357-5
ISBN-10 1-84078-357-5

Contents

11 Better Network Connections 153

12 Fixing Your PC 161

Index 187

1 Before You Start

This chapter is an introduction to the subject of computer upgrading and fixing, and offers some general advice on issues you should consider before you start pulling your PC to pieces.

Hot tip

If you are capable of wielding a screwdriver, you are capable of upgrading any part in a computer.

Don't forget

Removing and installing parts is easy. Getting the right part is not quite so easy, and thus a major part of this book is devoted to making sure you get this right.

Introduction

Given the pace at which computer technology is advancing, upgrading parts as they become obsolete is the only realistic way of having a PC that's capable of handling the latest software and hardware. Many people though, are wary of delving inside the system case for various reasons. These include: a) ignorance of what lies within, b) fear of invalidating warranties, and c) fear of damaging the PC. So they take the PC to a computer store and put up with the inconvenience and cost.

However, it is a fact that the physical act of replacing a computer part is very easy to do and is something that absolutely anyone is capable of. This book provides you with all the information you need, plus illustrated guides on how to install every component in the PC.

This is actually the easy bit, though. Getting the right parts for your purpose and making sure they are compatible with your existing setup is a lot more difficult and is something that does require some knowledge. For example, say you are replacing the hard drive: these devices are supplied with various interfaces, e.g. SATA and SCSI. Both of these have their pros and cons, which make them suitable for some setups and less so for others. Which will be the right one for your PC?

To make sure you make the right choices, you will find detailed descriptions of all the computer's parts and relevant specifications. This is extremely important as incorrect decisions may result, at best, in a PC that doesn't do what you wanted or expected it to, and at worst, that doesn't work at all.

There is also the issue of setting up of devices. With some, such as a sound card, this is straightforward but with others there is a lot more involved. For example, hard drives need to be partitioned and formatted before they can be used. Other parts require settings in the BIOS to be altered. Everything you need to know in these respects is explained.

Upgrades don't always go to plan and sometimes the new part won't work. If it's an essential system component, the PC itself might not work. To cover this, we provide a troubleshooting chapter that will help you to resolve most types of fault.

Is an Upgrade Necessary?

Before you decide to replace a component, make quite sure that it actually needs to be replaced. Some can appear to be malfunctioning when in reality the problem lies elsewhere, and others can be rejuvenated in various ways. The following are some typical examples:

- Hard drive performance can be seriously affected by a process known as fragmentation. So if you suspect that yours has a problem, you should always try defragmenting it first. These devices can also develop bad sectors, which can be the cause of data loss. Running the Windows disk repair utility will fix this

- When it comes to the speed of the PC, many people are fixated with the CPU – they think upgrading this part is guaranteed to give the system a boost. While it will to a certain extent, it is a fact that adding more memory will usually have a more significant impact

- Many devices have a flash upgradable chip (known as firmware), and most manufacturers provide firmware updates on their websites that reprogram these chips with a set of new instructions. Not only do the updates repair bugs, they often also add new features to the device in question. Check the manufacturers' websites to see if there are any worthwhile updates available for your devices before you replace them

- CD and DVD drives have a focal lens inside them that is used to focus the laser beam with which they read data. This lens can become contaminated by airborne pollutants resulting in inability to read discs, and even crashes and freezing of the PC. Before you replace the drive, try a lens cleaning kit

So unless you like spending money and making unnecessary work for yourself, see if there's a way to extend the life of existing parts.

Don't forget

Before buying a new hard drive for extra storage, try clearing your existing drive of redundant data. You may be surprised at how much space can be reclaimed by a good spring-clean.

Hot tip

Devices that can be improved by a flash upgrade include video cards, BIOS chips, CD/DVD drives, printers and modems.

Buying Options

Having decided to buy a new part, the upgrader has two choices – retail or OEM. Both have their pros and cons.

A retail boxed CPU. The package includes the processor, heatsink/fan assembly, warranty and full instructions.

Retail
A retail product comes fully packaged in a printed box, and with a user manual, registration card and a full warranty. In many cases, bundled software will be included as well. You will also get everything needed to get the device into operation. For example, buy a CPU and a heatsink/fan assembly will be supplied as well.

The most important thing, however, is that the product is more likely to be the genuine article – it is a fact that the computer parts market is flooded with counterfeit products of dubious origin (usually from the eastern hemisphere countries).

The disadvantage of buying retail products is that they cost more.

OEM
OEM is short for "Original Equipment Manufacturer". The term is used to describe a company that manufactures products to be sold under another company's brand name. These companies (typically, big computer manufacturers, such as Dell), buy large numbers of the various parts, put them together and then sell the finished computer under their own name.

An OEM CPU. This comes in a plain cardboard box and with the minimum of accessories, i.e. none.

OEM products also find their way on to the open market and can be bought from all the main outlets. The big advantage is that they are considerably cheaper than retail versions. However, there is a reason for this: they are sold in a plain box with no manual or bundled software, and usually with a limited warranty (typically, 30-60 days).

Also, very often, they will not be the complete article. For example, a retail hard drive will include the interface cables. OEM versions will not; you get the hard drive but nothing else.

So if you want to save money, buying OEM is the way to do it. Just remember that you will get no instructions, a limited warranty, and possibly an inferior product to boot. If you want guaranteed quality and all the "bells and whistles", buy a retail product.

Sourcing Your Parts

Retail Outlets

Buying from a computer store is the quickest and safest method. If the part is faulty or you buy the wrong one by mistake, you can simply take it back and get a replacement.

Their main drawback is price. Stores have high overheads to pay and so charge high prices. Also, the staff in these places are often not too knowledgeable regarding the products they are selling. If you need good (and honest) advice, it may not be forthcoming.

The large chain-stores are the worst in these respects. Smaller, specialist computer stores are better and will usually offer good and impartial advice. Prices may not be any lower (they may even be higher) but the quality of service is usually superior.

Mail-Order

The beauty of mail-order is that it enables buyers to compare prices without having to trudge around different stores. Also, sales staff are generally more clued-up than they are in stores.

The main advantage though, is that prices will be considerably less than in stores.

The Internet

Just about every product under the sun can be bought online these days and computer parts are no exception.

There are many websites that specialize in this area: two good examples of which are www.dabs.com in the UK and www.newegg.com in the USA (shown left).

Goods bought online will be cheaper than anywhere else. A further advantage is that online catalogs usually offer much more information, e.g. product specifications, than mail-order catalogs.

Beware

A common scam in retail stores is selling OEM products at the full retail price. Don't fall for this; if the product isn't supplied in the manufacturer's box, don't buy it unless you can negotiate a substantial discount.

Beware

Internet retailers are not above a few scams of their own. So don't buy anything from a site that doesn't provide a contact telephone number. Emails can be ignored; persistent calls can't be.

Precautions

If you follow the instructions in this book, you should encounter no difficulties as a result of any upgrades that are made. If you don't, or inadvertently damage a component, you could have real problems.

One of these, potentially, is loss of data. While we're not saying that this is likely, it is a possibility. Therefore, you are strongly advised to make a backup of any data on the PC that you do not wish to lose before you get started.

To do it, you will need a backup medium (a CD/DVD writer, a second hard drive or a Rev drive), and possibly a backup program as well depending on the level of backup.

The simplest method is to go through the hard drive methodically and copy the required data to the backup medium. The problem with this way of doing it is that it is very easy to miss stuff. Unless you are an organized type of person, and thus know exactly where everything is, you may not back up everything you need to.

A safer way is to back it all up. In this case, you will need a backup program, such as the one supplied by Windows (see margin note).

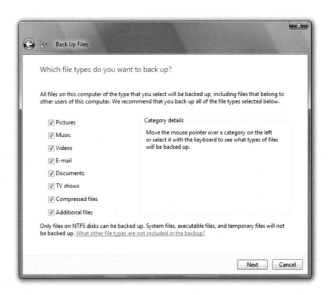

With this program (and others of its type), you can do a complete or selective backup.

Hot tip

Don't forget to back up items such as Internet favorites, emails, etc.

Beware

The various versions of Windows all supply a backup program. However, the one supplied with XP Home is not installed by default; you have to do it manually from the CD.

- Open the installation disc and click the following folders: VALUEADD, MSFT, NTBACKUP

- Click the NTBACKUP file to install the utility

- To access it, go to Start, All Programs, Accessories, System Tools, Backup

2 Discovering Your PC

The most crucial aspect of upgrading is ensuring the new device is compatible with the rest of the system. We explain how to get detailed information on every part in the computer.

Inside the Computer

Power supply unit (PSU)

Motherboard

Random Access Memory (RAM)

Central processing unit and heatsink/fan assembly

Expansion cards

PCI sockets

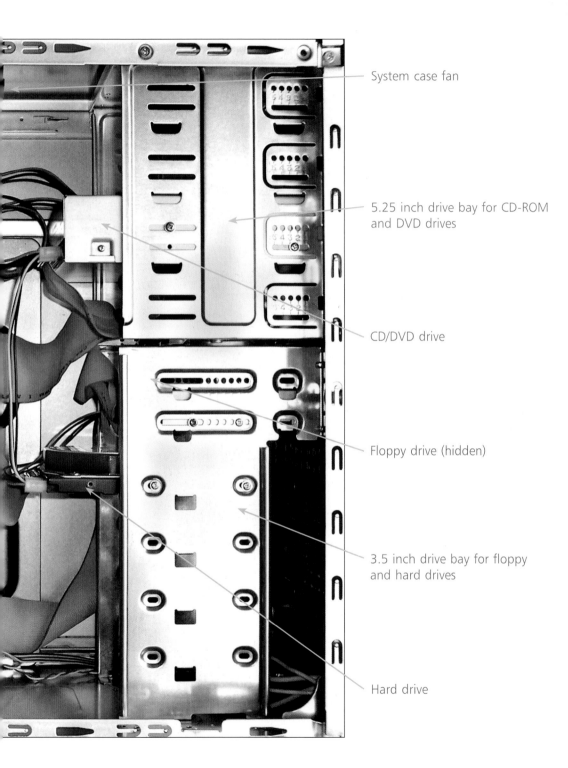

System case fan

5.25 inch drive bay for CD-ROM and DVD drives

CD/DVD drive

Floppy drive (hidden)

3.5 inch drive bay for floppy and hard drives

Hard drive

Outside the Computer

Power supply unit on/off switch

PS/2 ports. The green one is for the mouse, the purple for the keyboard

Serial port. This is obsolete but is provided for backward compatibility

USB ports. USB is the standard type of connection

Video card VGA output to the monitor

Modem socket for connection to the telephone line

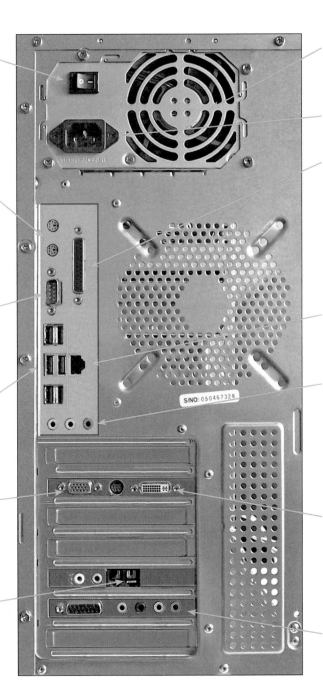

Power supply unit fan air intake

Power cord socket

Parallel port socket.
Used for parallel port devices such as older printers, scanners and Zip drives

LAN (local area network) socket

Motherboard audio sockets. Pink is for a microphone green is line out, and blue is line in

Video card DVI output to the monitor

Sound card audio sockets. The socket at the far left is a MIDI port

The Motherboard

Ports CPU socket Memory slots ATX Power connector BIOS chip

PCI slot AGP video card slot Chipset Floppy drive ATA socket ATA drive sockets SATA drive sockets

Motherboard Sockets

Every component in a computer system is connected to the motherboard. To facilitate this, these boards provide sockets, or slots, of various types.

Video Card Sockets

Video cards use either the Advanced Graphics Port (AGP) interface (older cards) or the PCI Express x16 interface (newer cards). These are high-speed buses that boost the performance of these cards considerably.

Note that PCI Express is a much faster interface than AGP and is the recommended option.

PCI Sockets

PCI sockets are used to connect other types of expansion card to the system. Most motherboards provide between three and five of these; some, however, may provide only one or two.

A recent extension of the PCI interface is PCI Express (see margin note), which offers much faster data transfer speeds. Increasingly, motherboards are now offering this new interface, usually with some PCI slots as well for backward compatibility.

Hot tip

Note that AGP sockets are always a different color to the white PCI and PCI Express sockets.

Hot tip

Unlike PCI, which uses a standard sized socket, the PCI Express interface uses sockets of various sizes – x1, x2, x4, x8, x12 and x16. The larger the socket, the higher the speed at which data is transferred.

PCI Express x16 socket (for video cards)

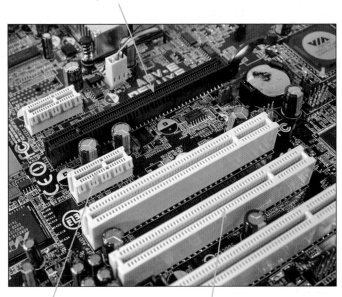

PCI Express x1 socket   PCI socket

Drive Sockets

The computer's drives (hard, floppy and CD/DVD) connect to the motherboard via either ATA or SATA interface sockets. ATA has been around for some twenty years and is still found on virtually all motherboards. However, it has now been superseded by the more recent SATA interface. As with PCI/PCI Express, SATA equipped motherboards also provide ATA sockets for backward compatibility.

Hot tip

Hard drive and CD/DVD drive ATA sockets are usually located on the right-hand side of the motherboard towards the middle. The floppy drive ATA socket is usually situated at the bottom of the board.

This motherboard provides both ATA and SATA connections

Ports

At the top-right of the motherboard are its input/output ports. These enable the user to connect peripheral devices to the system without having to open up the system case.

Most current motherboards provide all the ports shown on page 16. So if you upgrade yours, your system should still be compatible with any devices you may have that use the old serial and parallel ports. Check it out though, because some do not.

19

CPU and Memory

The PC's processor (the CPU) and its memory (RAM) are both located on the motherboard and, as far as the upgrader is concerned, they are the most important of its parts.

CPU

The CPU plugs into the motherboard via a large square socket that is usually located towards the top of the board (in ATX motherboards, which most are). Mounted on top of the CPU is a heatsink/fan assembly, which keeps the device cool. In operation, therefore, the CPU is not visible.

CPU hidden by the heatsink/fan assembly

Heatsink/fan assembly removed revealing the CPU

Memory (RAM)

Computer memory consists of a number of semiconductor chips mounted on an oblong circuit board. These circuit boards, or RAM modules as they are known, plug into a socket on the motherboard, which is usually situated to the left of the CPU. Most motherboards provide several of these sockets.

Don't forget

Memory sockets are usually situated at the top of the motherboard on the right-hand side.

Memory module installed in one of three available sockets on the motherboard

Expansion Cards

Expansion cards do what their name suggests – they expand the capabilities of a computer. They connect to the motherboard via its PCI or PCI Express sockets.

The most common of these are:

- Video cards
- Sound cards
- Modems

The easiest way of identifying them is by their input and output sockets.

Hot tip

Most hardware devices are also available as external models. In this case they will connect to the PC via its ports, usually, USB.

Video cards have either a blue VGA socket or a white DVI socket, or both. They are unmistakable in any case due to their large fans and heat sinks

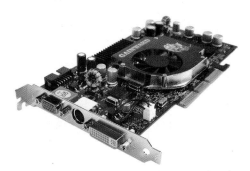

Hot tip

Another method of identifying expansion cards (assuming they are actually connected) is to follow the cable to the connected device. If it leads to the monitor, it has to be either the video card or the motherboard's integrated video system. If it's the speakers, it has to be the sound card or the integrated sound system. If it leads to the telephone jack, it has to be the modem.

Sound cards have a number of colored sockets, usually blue, green, black and orange. The sockets are often stamped as Mic, Line in, Line out, etc

Dial-up modems are small boards and usually have a single socket for connection to the telephone line. Voice enabled modems will also have Mic and Speaker sockets

Drive Units

All PCs have a hard drive and either a CD-ROM, or CD/DVD writer drive. Many also have a floppy drive. More recent PCs may have a CD writer and a DVD writer as well (or a single combination device that writes to both types of disc).

These devices are all located in the drive cages at the front of the system case, as shown below.

CD/DVD Drive

Floppy Drive

Hard Drive

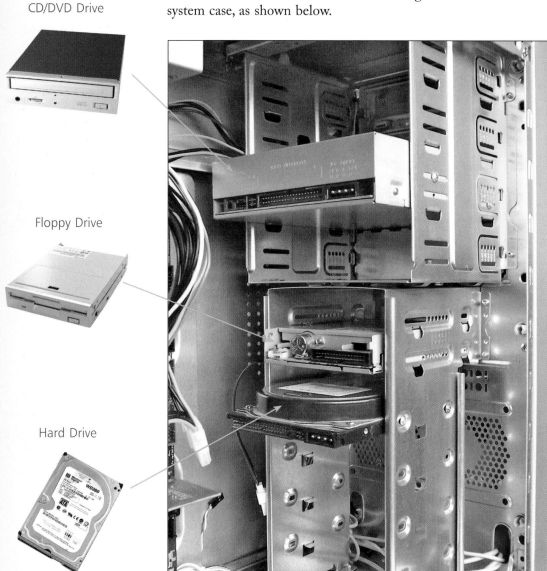

System Details

When replacing or adding a new component to your PC, you need to know some relevant details. The following are some typical examples:

- You've decided to upgrade your video card to a PCI Express model (or add one). However, before you do this, you need to know if your motherboard supports PCI Express

- Your PC is running slowly and you suspect that more memory is needed. Before you go out and buy some though, you will need to find out how much you currently have, and also what type of memory it is

- You decide to flash upgrade your BIOS. For this operation to be successful, it is essential that you know the model numbers of both the BIOS chip and the motherboard

If you still have the manual that came with the PC, all the required information should be available from it. If you don't though, you need another source. Your first port of call will be Windows itself.

All versions of this operating system provide a system information utility (see margin note) called System Information. This will tell you many things about your PC, one of which is details of all its hardware devices.

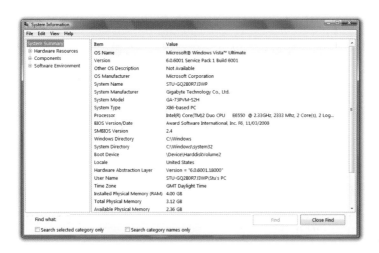

...cont'd

Don't forget

SiSoft Sandra is available at www.sisoftware. net. You will find four versions of this useful utility. The one that's free is the Lite version. Not all the modules are enabled with this version but the ones you need are.

However, while System Information is undoubtedly useful, there are many third-party system information utilities that tell you a great deal more about your computer. One of these is SiSoft Sandra, a free version of which is available for download from the Internet (see margin note).

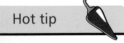

Hot tip

There are many system information tools available for free download from the Internet. Go to any software download site, such as www.download. com, and type "system information" in the search box.

SiSoft Sandra consists of a number of modules, each of which relate to a specific part of the system

In this example we are looking at the motherboard module. As you can see from the size of the scrollbar, there is a tremendous amount of information available here

This utility is highly recommended and will give you all the information you need about your system.

3 A Faster PC

The components that most influence the speed at which a computer runs are the CPU and the memory. Both of them are available in a range of models, each with specifications and features that make them suitable for certain applications. In this chapter, we show how to make sure the parts you buy are correct for your purposes.

Is a CPU Upgrade Necessary?

The usual reason for upgrading a CPU is to make the PC faster, and most people expect to see an immediate and significant improvement by doing so. However, it doesn't necessarily work like this.

For example, say, a 1.9 GHz CPU is replaced with a 3.8 GHz model; you may think that this will double the speed of the PC and that everything will happen twice as fast.

Unfortunately, it won't. While the PC will undoubtedly be more responsive, it won't bootup in half the time, programs will not open twice as quickly, etc. The extra processing capacity will become apparent only when an application that actually needs it is run. Whereas before, the PC may have struggled to cope, now it will run effortlessly.

So if your current CPU can handle your applications comfortably, upgrading it will make no significant difference to the performance of your PC (it would be like driving an Indy car in rush hour traffic – plenty of power but no way of using it).

However, should you develop an interest in any of the following, a CPU upgrade may well be what the doctor ordered:

- Video applications of any type. For example, movie-editing, 3D rendering, and animation, etc

- Computer Aided Design (CAD)

- Server applications

- High-level PC gaming. (Note that a mid-range CPU will run most games reasonably well. But if you want to play them with all the graphic and sound effects at maximum levels, a top-end CPU is essential)

Running these types of application on a system with anything other than a high-end CPU will have you banging your head on the desktop in frustration. As this is not going to do the desktop any good, you need to start looking at what's available in the CPU market.

Beware

Do not be taken in by the marketing hype surrounding CPUs. It is a fact that most home systems run perfectly well with a low- to mid-range model.

Hot tip

Before replacing your CPU, try installing extra memory. In most cases, this will make a greater improvement to the PC's performance than a CPU upgrade will.

The CPU Market

The CPU you buy will be from one of two manufacturers – AMD or Intel. There are others but these two companies dominate the Desktop PC processor market.

Intel

For many years Intel CPUs were to be found in virtually all computers and, even today, it still has the lion's share particularly in the corporate and high-end Desktop market.

Like its rival AMD, it manufactures a range of CPUs that are designed to suit all pockets and requirements. These are as follows:

Starting at the top, Intel's flagship CPUs are the dual-core Itanium 2 and the quad-core Xeon, both of which are designed for the corporate and server markets where very high levels of performance are required. They are also very highly priced. For the home user, they have little relevance.

Next up are the quad-core Core 2 and dual-core Core 2 series of CPUs. The latter is currently Intel's most popular class of CPU. There is also a dual-core Pentium, which will also be of interest to the upgrader.

Hot tip

Dual-core CPUs are currently the most popular type of processor.

Courtesy of Intel Corporation

At the bottom of the Intel range is the Celeron. This CPU is basically a Pentium 4 with a much lower specification. Even so, it is a fact that these CPUs are adequate for most purposes. At the time of writing, a new dual-core Celeron has just been released by Intel.

AMD (Advanced Micro Devices)

With their Athlon class of CPU, AMD captured a large chunk of Intel's share of the Desktop PC market. This was due mainly to the fact that the Athlon cost less than the Intel equivalent (the Pentium 4) while still delivering the same level of performance. This made them very popular with the PC manufacturers.

However, the pendulum has now swung the other way as Intel's dual-core CPUs are generally considered to be superior to AMD's dual-core offerings.

AMD's top of the range CPU is the quad-core Opteron, and this processor is aimed at the corporate and server markets where it competes with Intel's Itanium and Xeon.

Next is the dual-core Athlon 64 X2 range, which is intended for mid- to high-end Desktop PCs. It competes with Intel's dual-core Core 2 CPUs.

This is followed by the single-core Athlon 64 CPU, which is an inexpensive option for those whose processing requirements are modest.

AMD's budget CPU is the Sempron (shown right). As with the Intel's Celeron, the Sempron is basically a stripped-down version of an existing CPU (the Athlon), and offers lower cache memory and FSB.

This CPU is also available in a 64-bit version, which is the most expensive in the Sempron range.

CPU Performance Ratings

AMD

AMD's original method was the source of much confusion to buyers. This was due to the fact that their CPUs ran at a lower clock speed than equivalents from Intel while still producing the same level of performance.

For example, an old 2.6 GHz Pentium 4 had a clock speed of 2.6 GHz. In terms of performance, the AMD equivalent was the 2600 Athlon. However, the clock speed of this CPU was actually 2.1 GHz, which was considerably less. Worried that if they advertised their CPUs at the true clock speed consumers would think they offered lower performance than Intel's, they introduced the performance rating.

However, with their new range of dual-core Athlon 64 CPUs, AMD have done away with the performance rating and are now advertising them at the true clock speed. For example, an Athlon 64 X2 6000+ AM2 has two cores each running at 3 GHz, which is indicated by the 6000+.

Hot tip

Probably the only rating that really needs to concern the buyer is the price. The more the CPU costs, the better it will perform.

Intel

Traditionally, Intel simply advertised their CPUs at the clock speed. However, they have now gone in the opposite direction to AMD and have introduced a rating system of their own. This removes references to specific specifications, such as clock speed and FSB, and replaces them with a three-digit number (735 in the example below).

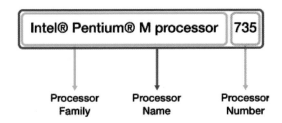

| Intel® Pentium® M processor | 735 |

Processor Family   Processor Name   Processor Number

Unfortunately, by itself, the number is actually completely meaningless. To derive any information from it, you will need to visit Intel's website at "www.intel.com/products/processor_number/info.htm".

Here you will find a list of all their CPUs, rating numbers and associated meanings.

What CPU Do You Need?

All computers can be placed in one of four categories: low-end, mid-range, high-end, and gaming machines. The CPU you buy will, to a large degree, be dictated by which of these categories your PC is in, or intended to be in.

High-End Systems
These systems are predominantly servers and workstations, which require the most powerful processors, i.e. Intel's Xeon and Itanium, and AMD's Opteron.

Home users requiring out-of-the-ordinary performance levels will be suitably served by one of the high-end dual core CPUs, such as AMD's Athlon 64 X2 6400+ and Intel's Core 2 Duo E6850.

For really extreme performance, a new family of quad-core Desktop CPUs are available from both Intel and AMD.

Mid-Range Systems
Home computers are mostly in this class of computer. These PCs tend to be used for a range of applications, some of which need a reasonably powerful CPU, and others of which don't. For example, PC games that aren't too CPU-intensive (not all of them are), office applications, email, and the Internet.

All of these will run very nicely with a low-end dual-core CPU. Examples are AMD's Athlon 64 X2 3800+ and Intel's Core 2 Duo E4500. Also suitable for the price-concious is the single-core Pentium E2140 (for as long as it is available).

Low-End Systems
Basic applications such as word-processing, playing simple games such as FreeCell, email, and web browsing require very little from the CPU. Single-core Athlon 64s and Semprons from AMD, and Celerons from Intel will be perfectly adequate here.

However, if you tend to run several of these simultaneously, a low-end dual-core model will be better.

Hot tip

An important factor to remember when upgrading your CPU is your possible requirements in the future. While you may not need a powerful one now, you may subsequently develop an interest that does require more processing power. For this reason, it makes sense to buy one with "a bit in hand".

High-Performance Gaming Machines

For the hardcore gamer, there can be no compromises – the PC is set up with one purpose in mind – playing 3D games with "all guns blazing".

To get the best out of these games in terms of frame rate (speed), and graphic and sound options, a seriously powerful CPU will be required.

AMD and Intel both supply CPUs designed specifically for gaming machines. Currently, Intel's offering is the Core 2 Extreme range of processors. These are quad-core models (dual-core models are also available at a more affordable price) that will play 3D games at the ultimate level.

AMD's is the Athlon FX series. These CPUs are available as both quad-core and dual-core models and deliver a similar level of processing power as Intel's Extreme range.

Hot tip

Note that the two CPUs mentioned opposite are currently the best choice for hardcore gamers. By the time you are reading this, however, the situation may have changed.

CPU Specifications

Now that you know what type of CPU is required in terms of performance, the next task is to choose one that will do the job. This means looking at the specifications, and the following are the ones that should be considered.

Clock Speed

This is the speed at which a CPU runs and is measured as a frequency, e.g. 20 MHz, or 20 million cycles per second. As every action carried out by the CPU requires one or more cycles, it follows that the higher the clock speed, the more instructions it will be able to process in any given second.

You need to be aware though, that clock speed is just one of several factors that determines a CPU's performance. We look at the others below.

Front Side Bus (FSB)

A very important CPU specification is the speed at which it communicates with the rest of the PC; this is commonly known as the Front Side Bus speed or FSB.

For example, you can have two CPUs rated at, say, 3 GHz. One has an FSB of 1066 MHz and the other has an FSB of 800 MHz. Although they both have the same processing power, the one with the higher FSB will perform better as it can transfer data at a much faster speed.

Thus, those of you who want a powerful PC will need a CPU with a high FSB (note that the FSB must be supported by the motherboard).

Currently, the fastest FSB is 1600 MHz and will be supported only by high-end motherboards. Mainstream motherboards, typically, support FSBs of 800 MHz, 1066 MHz and 1333 MHz.

Cache Memory

Cache memory is an area of high-speed memory within the CPU, which is used to store frequently accessed data. Because this data doesn't have to be retrieved from the much slower memory, overall performance is improved considerably.

A CPU with a 2 MB cache and the same clock speed as a similar CPU with a 1 MB cache will perform much better.

Other factors to consider, include:

Compatibility

The CPU connects to the PC via a socket on the motherboard. However, different processors use different types of socket, so you must establish that your chosen CPU is physically compatible with the socket on your motherboard (see page 53). Also, be aware that motherboards are built for either Intel or AMD CPUs – they are not interchangeable.

Cooling

CPUs generate a lot of heat and so must be adequately cooled by a suitable heatsink/fan assembly to prevent them from burning out. If you buy a retail CPU, this won't be a problem – an approved unit will be included.

However, if you buy an OEM product, you will have to buy one separately. The important thing here is to make sure that the heatsink/fan assembly you buy is recommended for use with the CPU. If it is not, you could well have problems down the line.

Power

This will be a consideration only if you are buying one of the latest high-end CPUs. These devices draw a lot of power, so you must make sure that the Power Supply Unit is up to the job (see page 126).

Technology

Intel and AMD both employ various technologies on certain types of their processors. These make a considerable difference to both the performance and the price of the CPUs in question. We'll look at these on the next page.

Hot tip

Note that CPUs commonly use two types of cache – L1 and L2. L2 is slightly slower than L1 but is larger.

CPU Technologies

Hyper-Transport
Hyper-Transport is a technology developed by AMD, which replaces the traditional CPU Front Side Bus with an optimized high-speed interconnection system. The result is faster communication between the CPU, memory and the motherboard chipset and, as a result, overall performance is much increased.

For the home user, the level of performance provided by Hyper-Transport is never likely to be needed except, perhaps, by those interested in a high-performance machine for gaming.

Multi-Core
Dual-core and quad-core CPUs have two or four processor cores respectively on the same chip. Each core functions and processes data independently, and they are coordinated by the operating system.

However, a performance-limiting factor is the fact that a multi-core CPU has to share hardware such as the memory controller and the front side bus. Thus, a multi-core system will never be as good as a multi-processor system in which totally independent CPUs are used, each of which has its own hardware.

64-Bit Architecture
This technology has been around for a while now but its take-up has been slow – see margin note. A 64-bit CPU can process data much more quickly than a 32-bit CPU, resulting in a much higher level of performance.

The main problem with 64-bit technology is that to gain the full advantages offered, software (including the operating system and hardware drivers) needs to be 64-bit compatible. So anyone upgrading to a 64-bit CPU will also need to buy a complete new set of software.

Note that existing 32-bit software will run on a 64-bit system but with no performance gain.

Beware

If you decide to upgrade your PC to a 64-bit system, you may be jumping the gun. Although 64-bit operating systems are available, software manufacturers are not exactly falling over themselves to follow suit.

The reason is that as very few users need the level of performance offered by 64-bit systems, sales of 64-bit software are likely to be very slow, initially.

Installing a CPU

Ideally, the motherboard will have been removed from the system case; not only does this make the procedure considerably easier but there is also less chance of damaging the motherboard.

That said, it is quite possible to do the job in situ as long as you exercise some care. However, with anything other than a mid- or full-tower system case (both of which give unrestricted access), you will have to first remove the power supply unit, as this device will impede access. You may also have to disconnect the CD/DVD, floppy, and hard drive interface cables.

1 The first step is to remove the existing CPU and heatsink/fan assembly. You will probably find that the two are welded together by thermal paste, in which case you will have to separate them by inserting a thin blade and prising them apart

2 Having removed the heatsink/fan assembly, lift the socket locking lever (illustrated below) and then remove the CPU

Socket locking lever

Hot tip

The procedure for installing CPUs is exactly the same for both Intel and AMD CPUs.

35

Beware

Beware of your body's electrostatic electricity when handling CPUs. Purchasing and using an electrostatic wriststrap is recommended.

...cont'd

Hot tip

Socket LGA775, which is used by Intel's dual-core CPUs, has the pins on the socket rather than on the CPU itself. The installation procedure is no different though.

3 Align the corner of the new CPU with the corresponding corner in the socket (see bottom margin note)

Hot tip

Different CPUs use different methods of ensuring the CPU is inserted the correct way up. Some have 2 pins removed from one corner and two holes removed from one corner of the socket. Or there may be a mark, such as a gold triangle, on the CPU and on the corresponding corner of the socket.

4 Drop the CPU into the socket

Hot tip

Unlike a memory module, a CPU does not require any pressure when being fitted. Simply align the pins with the holes and it will drop into place. Note that the pins are very easily bent so a degree of care is needed.

5 Close the socket's locking lever

Hot tip

Make sure the CPU is fitted correctly (all four sides must be flush with the socket) before you close the locking lever. Otherwise, you will bend and possibly break some of the pins.

Installing a Heatsink/Fan Assembly

Beware

New heatsinks are supplied with a thermal pad in situ, as shown below. Be careful to keep your fingers off it as dead skin and oil reduces its effectiveness.

It is extremely important that thermal compound is placed between the heatsink and the CPU. This greatly improves heat transfer and if it isn't done, the CPU will either soon burn out or run at a temperature that makes it (and thus the PC) unstable.

There are two methods of fixing heatsink/fan assemblies:

1)   Clip assembly/retention frame
2)   Clips that loop over the heatsink/fan assembly

Clip Assembly/Retention Frame

Fixed to the motherboard is a retention frame as shown below.

Don't forget

If you are reusing an existing heatsink, you will have to remove the old thermal paste with a suitable solvent and then replace it with new paste. This is available from any computer store in the form of either pads or a tube of thermal paste.

Mounted on the heatsink itself is a clip assembly, which engages with the retention frame.

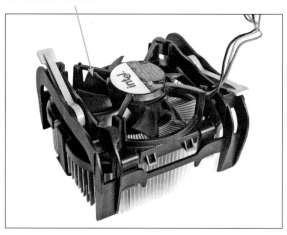

1 Align the heatsink with the retention frame and simply press down; it should snap into place

2 Swing the two locking levers through 180 degrees to lock the heatsink in place. Finally, connect the CPU fan to the motherboard

Beware

Aligning the heatsink with the retention frame so that the retaining clips are in the right place on all four sides can be somewhat fiddly. Once done though, it snaps into place easily.

Don't forget

Don't forget to close the assembly locking levers; this is something that is easily overlooked.

Clips

Heatsink/fan assemblies secured by clips can be a bit more tricky to fit as some force may required to engage the clips.

1 Check that there is a thermal strip or paste on the bottom of the heatsink

2 Align the heatsink with the socket

3 Engage the locking clip on one side of the heatsink over the matching lug on the socket (or motherboard)

Hot tip

When engaging the locking clips, hold the heatsink steady. If it slips about, the thermal compound will smear all over the place.

4 Engage the clip on the other side of the heatsink (or motherboard). You may need a flat-head screwdriver to force it into place

Hot tip

The CPU's fan power supply will be on the motherboard in the vicinity of the CPU. It is a 3-pin socket and is labeled "CPU Fan".

5 Connect the CPU's fan to the motherboard's CPU fan power supply. Don't forget to do this because if you don't the CPU will burn out very quickly

When is a Memory Upgrade Necessary?

When you buy a PC, it will come with an adequate amount of memory to run the operating system and software installed on it. However, as the memory requirements of both software and hardware increase with every succeeding version and model, the time will inevitably come when you no longer have enough.

When your PC slows to an unacceptable level when running an application (or a number of applications simultaneously), the time for a memory upgrade has come.

The amount that you need depends on your operating system (all operating systems need a minimum amount to function properly), the type of applications you run, and the number of applications that you run simultaneously (multi-tasking). The following table gives a rough guide:

Operating System	Low Usage	Mid Usage	High Usage
Windows Vista	500 MB	1 GB	2 GB
Windows XP	256 MB	512 MB	1 GB
Windows Me	128 MB	256 MB	512 MB
Mac OS X	128 MB	256 MB	512 MB
Linux	80 MB	140 MB	212 MB

Low usage is defined as resource-light applications, such as word-processing, web browsing, email, 2D games, data entry, etc. If you tend to run several of these applications simultaneously, you should install the amount specified in the Mid usage column.

Mid usage is running programs such as photo-editing, web applications, desktop publishing, sound-editing, printing, scanning, etc. If you run several of these at the same time, install the amount specified in the High usage column.

High usage is defined as 3D gaming (particularly online gaming), real-time video-editing, computer aided design (CAD), animation, 3D modeling, etc.

Types of Memory

There are three types of memory in mainstream use at the moment:

1) DDR SDRAM
2) DDR2 SDRAM
3) DDR3 SDRAM

DDR is the oldest of the three and has now been superceded by DDR2. However, it is still found on millions of PCs around the world and is still a perfectly good type of memory.

Next is DDR2 (an enhanced version of DDR), which is currently the type in favor and will be found on the vast majority of new PCs.

DDR3 is an enhancement of DDR2 and has only been on the market for a few months.

DDR SDRAM

In comparison to its predecessor (SDR SDRAM), DDR SDRAM transfers data much more quickly due to a technical modification whereby data is transferred on both the up and down sides of a clock cycle as opposed to just one side. The table below lists the various versions that are available:

Version	Clock Speed (MHz)	FSB Speed (MHz)	Transfer Rate (GB/s)
PC1600	100	100	1.6
PC2100	133	133	2.1
PC2400	150	150	2.4
PC2700	166	166	2.7
PC3200	200	200	3.2

All three types are available in standard versions for mainstream use and high-performance versions (shown below) designed for gamers and power users.

DDR2 SDRAM

DDR2 operates the external data bus twice as fast as DDR. This is achieved by improved bus signaling, and by operating the memory cells at half the clock rate (one quarter of the data transfer rate), rather than at the clock rate as with DDR.

These modules have a 240-pin edge connector, so they are incompatible with motherboards designed for DDR modules, which use 184-pin sockets. DDR2 is currently available in the following versions:

Version	Clock Speed (MHz)	FSB Speed (MHz)	Data Transfer Rate (GB/s)
PC2-3200	100	200	3.2
PC2-4300	133	266	4.3
PC2-5400	166	333	5.4
PC2-6400	200	400	6.4
PC2-8500	266	533	8.5

DDR3 SDRAM

DDR3 modules can transfer data at 800–1600 MHz as opposed to 400-800 MHz with DDR2 and 200-400 MHz with DDR. DDR3 also uses up to 30 per cent less power than DDR2. DDR3 is currently available in the following versions:

Version	Clock Speed (MHz)	FSB Speed (MHz)	Data Transfer Rate (GB/s)
PC3-6400	100	400	6.4
PC3-8500	133	533	8.5
PC3-10600	166	667	10.6
PC3-12800	200	800	12.8

DDR3 modules have a 240-pin edge connector as with DDR2 modules but the key notch is in a different location. This means that they can only be used in a motherboard designed for DDR3.

Error Checking Modules

When investigating the memory market, you will also come across other, apparently different types of memory, such as Parity, ECC, etc. We'll take a brief look at these.

Parity
Parity modules have an extra (parity) chip for error detection. This checks that data is correctly read or written by the memory module by adding additional bits and using a special algorithm. However, it will not correct an error.

ECC
ECC modules are very similar to Parity modules. However, unlike Parity modules, the ECC module will, in most cases, correct any errors it finds depending on the type of error.

Buffered
Buffered modules contain a buffer chip to help the module cope with the large electrical load required for large amounts of memory. The buffer electrically isolates the memory from the controller to minimize the load on the chipset.

Registered
Very similar to Buffered memory, these modules contain registers that hold the data for one clock cycle before it is moved on to the motherboard.

All of the above modules are based on SDRAM technology. The difference between them and standard SDRAM memory is the fact that they incorporate some type of error checking technique that increases their reliability (and hence that of the PC) considerably.

For this reason they are found predominantly in Servers and mission-critical systems. The typical home PC has no need for these types of memory.

Drawbacks are that they are considerably more expensive, and are also slower in operation (due to the error checking procedure).

Don't forget

The types of memory described on this page are not intended for use in a typical home PC. The only users who might have a need for them are those who do mission-critical work on their PC.

Buying Memory

When the time comes to make this decision, you should have already decided what type of system you want, i.e. low-, mid-, high-end or gaming, and chosen your motherboard and CPU accordingly. This is important, as to get the best out of your memory it must be compatible with these devices.

You need to consider the following:

Type of Memory

This is the first thing to decide and is a straightforward decision: DDR, DDR2 or DDR3.

While technically it is now obsolete, DDR is still readily available for users who simply want to replace a damaged module or add extra memory without also changing their motherboard (as would be the case if they wanted to fit DDR2 or DDR3).

DDR2 is cheap, fast, and compatible with mainstream motherboards. For low- to mid-level systems, it is the obvious choice. If you are building a gaming or high-performance machine, go for the souped-up modules, such as Corsair's XMS and Kingston's Hyper-X.

If you want to be at the cutting-edge then the new DDR3 SDRAM will be a consideration. DDR3 will ensure that your system is future-proofed as far as possible in relation to memory

Just bear in mind that it is very expensive and the current models suffer from low timings, which means they perform little better than DDR2. This will change with later models but for now it may be better to stick to DDR2.

Whichever type you go for, if you need the highest possible level of reliability, you will need to buy error checking modules as discussed on page 45.

Don't forget

For typical computer uses, you need look no further than DDR2 SDRAM. Performance enthusiasts will consider high-performance modules such as Kingston's Hyper-X. Cutting-edge enthusiasts will be interested in DDR3 memory.

Front Side Bus (FSB)

For the best possible system performance, the memory's FSB must be the same as the CPU's, otherwise it becomes a performance bottleneck. However, modern dual-core CPUs have high FSBs, typically, 1300 MHz and the fastest mainstream DDR2 memory, PC2-8500, has an FSB of only 533 MHz. So what are your options? There are three:

1) Buy a PC3-12800 DDR3 module. This has an FSB of 800 MHz, which closes the gap considerably

2) Use dual-channel memory. This requires a dual-channel enabled motherboard and a matched pair of identical memory modules. This will achieve a memory speed increase of about 10-15 per cent

3) Settle for a trade-off in terms of cost versus performance

The memory's FSB also needs to be supported by the motherboard. The easiest way to ensure you get this right is to look at the motherboard's specifications, which you will find at the relevant manufacturers' website. An example is shown below:

Beware

If you install a memory module rated at a speed higher than the motherboard and CPU are designed to handle, the memory will still work but only at the motherboard's maximum FSB. You won't be getting the best out of it.

If you install a module rated at a speed lower than the motherboard or CPU FSB, this will create a bottleneck in the system as the memory will not be able to keep up. The result will be degraded system performance.

Intel® Desktop Board D915PBL Features	
Form Factor	ATX (12" x 9.6 " [304.8 mm by 243.84 mm])
Processor	• Support for the Intel® Pentium® 4 processor with Hyper-Threading Technology (including Extreme Edition) in the LGA 775 socket with a 800 MHz system bus • Supports boxed Intel desktop processors with packaging designated by 04B or 04A Platform Compatibility Guide.
Memory	• Four 240-pin DIMM connectors supporting up to four double-sided DIMMs • DDR2 533/400 SDRAM memory • Designed to support up to 4 GB^2 of system memory
Chipset	Intel® 915P Express Chipset
I/O Control	Integrated super I/O LPC bus controller
Audio	Intel® High Definition Audio, combined with Intel® Audio Studio, delivers premium 8-channel audio that rivals discrete add card solutions. • Five configurable back panel ports • One optical out port • One Coaxial out port (analog)
Video	PCI Express* x16 connector (with integrated retention mechanism) provides enhanced bandwidth for next-generation graphics card technology and future headroom.
Peripheral Interfaces	• Up to eight Hi-Speed USB 2.0 ports • Up to three IEEE 1394a ports • Four Serial ATA IDE ports featuring Intel® Matrix Storage Technology with RAID 0, 1, and 0+1 support. • One ATA-66/100 and UDMA-33 connector • PS/2* keyboard and mouse ports • One parallel port • One serial port

Don't forget

To work in dual-channel mode, the modules must be identical (many memory manufacturers sell dual-channel kits for this purpose). Dual-channel must also be supported by both the motherboard and CPU.

The specs show you the type, speed, and amount of memory supported by the board.

cont'd

Another method is to use the online configurator tools provided by the memory manufacturers.

The following example is from Corsair at www.corsairmemory.com (access to the configurator is on the home page).

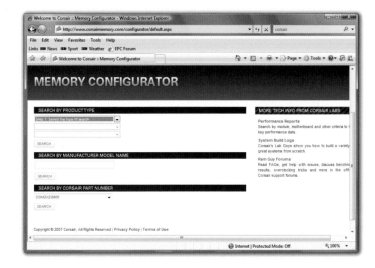

Memory configurator

This lets you search by system or by memory module. For example, you can enter your existing system details (manufacturer, model, etc) and see what memory is available for the system.

Speed

While you can install a memory module of any speed in your system, it will only run at the rated speed if that speed is supported by the motherboard. For example, if you install a PC4000 module, which runs at 500 MHz in a motherboard whose maximum memory speed is 400 MHz, the module will run at 400 MHz, so you won't be getting the best out of it. Don't forget to check this out in the specifications.

Capacity

The amount of memory that can be installed in a system is dictated by the motherboard. Currently, most mainstream motherboards will support 2 GB. For typical home users this is more than enough. Only gamers and power-users are likely to need more than this level of capacity.

How to Install Memory

Installing new or extra memory is one of the easiest upgrades. Do it as follows:

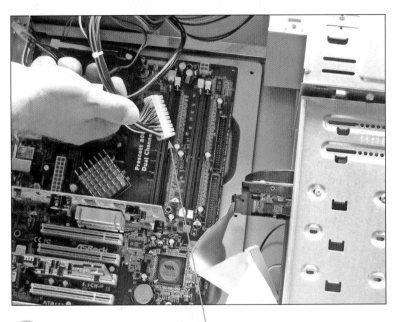

Beware

Of all the components in a PC, memory modules are the ones most likely to be damaged by electrostatic electricity. So before handling one, ground yourself by touching something metal. Then pick it up by the edges.

1   Disconnect or move any cables that are obstructing access to the memory sockets

2   Find the lowest numbered socket (each one is numbered at the ends) and open the retaining clips

Hot tip

When upgrading memory, you will get the best results if you put the module in the lowest numbered socket. Typically, they are labeled 0, 1, 2, 3, etc, with socket zero being the lowest. If there are no labels on the motherboard, the socket closest to the CPU should be considered to be socket 0.

3   Align the edge connector cut-out with the lug on the socket

...cont'd

4 Ease the module into the socket

5 Press down firmly at both ends

6 When the module is correctly seated, the retaining clips will close automatically

4 A More Versatile PC

To make a PC more versatile it is necessary to add to its existing capabilities. As these are inherent to the motherboard, doing so often requires that this device be upgraded as well. There are many factors that will influence this decision and this chapter ensures that you will make the correct one.

Is an Upgrade Necessary?

There are three reasons to upgrade a motherboard:

1) The existing one has failed

2) You want a more powerful PC

3) To modernize your system

However, this is not the easiest of tasks as it can mean literally stripping the system down to gain access to the board, and then rebuilding it. Also, because so many other parts are involved, the potential for something going wrong as a result is higher than with any other type of upgrade.

These are two good reasons to not do it unless absolutely necessary. Another is that a motherboard upgrade may require other components to be upgraded as well.

The older your system, the more likely this is. Vintage PCs (ten years, or more, old), will be incompatible with modern motherboards in virtually every respect. Even the case may need replacing. In this situation, a brand new PC makes more sense than a motherboard upgrade.

With systems between five and ten years old, the CPU and memory will almost certainly have to be replaced. It is also quite likely that some expansion cards (notably modems and sound cards), will be using the old, and now obsolete, ISA interface. Video cards, however, will probably be PCI models, and thus re-usable.

A motherboard upgrade to accommodate a modern CPU could mean a new power supply unit as well. This is due to the high power requirements of these devices. It would be absolute folly to run one of the latest and greatest CPUs on an old 300 watt PSU; it would probably blow immediately, taking your new CPU with it.

The bottom line then, is that before you do it be sure that there is no alternative. Clearly, if the existing board has failed, it's a no-brainer. If it's a faster PC you want, try a memory upgrade first. If you need support for new technology, check that it can't be added to the existing motherboard in the form of a PCI card.

Hot tip

Anyone intending to upgrade their PC is well advised to take a good look at what's available in the motherboard field. While we can only scratch the surface here, there are many websites that provide detailed analysis of the latest boards.

Beware

In most cases, a motherboard upgrade means more than just replacing the board. Other devices will have to be replaced as well.

Buying a Motherboard

Because the motherboard is the central component in the PC, replacing it with a different model can, and often does, have ramifications with regard to other components in the PC.

Compatibility Issues

All PC hardware needs to be compatible with the motherboard, both in terms of technology, and method of connection. The most important are the CPU and memory.

CPU

The first consideration with the CPU is physical compatibility with the motherboard. This means that the board must have the socket that the CPU was designed for. A quick look at the specifications will ensure you get this right. The CPU specs will specify the socket required – socket AM2, 939, 775, etc. The motherboard specs will specify the socket provided.

The next consideration is the range of FSB speeds supported by the motherboard. Ideally, it will provide one that is the same as the CPU's FSB. However, it's not critical if it doesn't. The system will still work but at the lower of the two speeds (see page 32 for more on this). Again, you need to look at the specifications.

Alternatively, use the system building guides provided by AMD (www.amd.com) and Intel (www.intel.com) on their websites. Just select the CPU you want and you will be presented with a list of compatible motherboards – it couldn't be easier.

Memory

The considerations with memory are similar to the CPU. Firstly, the module has to be physically compatible, and secondly, its rated speed should be supported by the motherboard.

A possible third factor is the maximum amount of memory supported by the board. However, with regard to the latter, it must be said that most boards support at least 2 GB of memory, so for most people this won't be an issue.

Hot tip

Many computer retail outlets supply kits, which comprise a matched motherboard, CPU and memory. This is an option for those who don't want the bother of matching the parts themselves.

Don't forget

Don't forget to check that the motherboard supports the CPU's clock speed.

...cont'd

This information is available from the motherboard's specifications, as shown below.

Memory	
Number of Slots	2
Number of Pins	184-Pin
Maximum Memory Supported	2GB
Memory Supported	DDR266 (PC2100) DDR333 (PC2700) DDR400 (PC3200)

This board can support 2 GB of DDR RAM at speeds ranging from 266 MHz to 400 MHz

Form Factors

A motherboard's form factor relates to its physical dimensions and needs to be matched to the form factor of the system case and the power supply unit. This ensures that they are all physically compatible with each other, i.e. they fit in the case and the screwholes line up.

The vast majority of PCs these days use the ATX form factor, which is available in three sizes – ATX, Mini ATX and Micro ATX. ATX motherboards are used in full- and mid-tower system cases, Mini ATX in mini system cases, while Micro ATX boards are used in Desktop system cases.

If your system is housed in a full- or mid-tower case, you can use a motherboard built to any variation of ATX, as these cases are downward compatible, i.e. they have mounting points for all of them. If you have a Desktop case, however, you will be restricted to a Micro ATX board.

Making sure you get the correct size of motherboard for your case is straightforward as they are all advertised with the form factor used. For example: ABIT KV7 Via Socket A ATX. This tells you the motherboard manufacturer (Abit), the chipset manufacturer (Via), the CPU socket type (Socket A) and the form factor (ATX).

Hot tip

A more recent PC form factor that was introduced in 2004 is BTX. One of the primary aims of BTX is to improve the level of cooling within the system case. This has become necessary due to the high levels of heat generated by the newer CPUs.

Be aware that if you decide to go the BTX route, you will also have to buy a BTX compatible motherboard. All other system components are compatible with BTX, however.

Motherboard Sockets

The motherboard's sockets allow you to expand and update your
system as and when required. It is crucial that the new board has
the right type, and also enough of them.

ISA

If your system dates back to the late 1990's, some of your devices
may use the ISA interface. As this is now obsolete, you will not
be able to use these devices with a modern motherboard. If this is
the case, a motherboard upgrade will require these devices to be
upgraded as well.

PCI

Currently, this is the standard interface for internal hardware
devices. The only thing you need to check here is that the
motherboard supplies enough PCI sockets for your devices.

PCI Express

This is an enhanced version of the PCI interface that is expected
to eventually supersede PCI. However, it is a fact that current
hardware is incapable of fully utilizing the extra bandwidth
provided by PCI Express, with the possible exception of video
cards. So for the vast majority of people, this new interface is not
necessary.

AGP

This socket is provided for AGP video cards. So if you have, or
intend to get, one of these cards, make sure the motherboard has
an AGP socket (not all do).

Note that the PCI Express interface also provides a socket (x16)
for video cards. Most of the top-end video cards are now using
this, so if hardcore gaming is your forte, you may want to make
sure that your motherboard has a x16 PCI Express socket.

Drive

The current standard interface for connecting drive units to the
system is SATA and all motherboards now provide this. However,
there are still many ATA drives in use so new motherboards also
provide this interface.

Hot tip

Even if you currently
have no PCI Express
devices, by buying a
PCI Express enabled
motherboard, your
system will be future-
proofed in this respect.

...cont'd

Integrated Hardware

Traditionally, built-in hardware has been restricted mainly to sound and video systems, neither of which offered much in the way of quality and features. For example, early integrated video did not have 3D capability, which is essential for the playing of 3D games, and the sound systems could only handle the two nasty little speakers that manufacturers, typically, supplied.

Today, the situation is much different. The sound systems now supplied with motherboards can support multiple-speaker setups, and the video systems have full 3D capabilities. For most users, these systems are more than adequate.

Quite apart from sound and video, motherboards offer a range of integrated hardware. These include: Ethernet and wireless network adaptors, modems, hardware firewalls and RAID hard drive controllers. The advantages these offer to the upgrader are:

- Reduced cost – for example, buying a motherboard with an integrated video system will cost much less than buying a motherboard and a separate video card

- Increased expansion options – if some of your hardware is built-in to the motherboard, you will have spare PCI sockets that would be otherwise occupied. These can be used for other devices

Technology

Whatever the reason for replacing a motherboard, the act of doing so presents an ideal opportunity to embrace more recent PC technologies at the same time. For example:

- CPU technology, such as multi-processors (see next page)

- System buses, such as SATA, PCI Express, USB2 and Bluetooth (see margin note)

- DDR2/DDR3 memory

Types of Motherboard

Dual-Processor Motherboards

A dual-processor motherboard has two CPU sockets, which allows two separate CPUs to be installed. These act independently of each other and have their own hardware support (as opposed to a dual-core CPU, where the system's hardware is shared).

The result, not surprisingly, is a significant boost in processing power. However, this type of setup comes at a price – an expensive dual-CPU motherboard, plus two CPUs. For home users, setups like this are overkill.

Dual-Channel Motherboards

These motherboards provide matched pairs of memory slots in which identical modules are installed. Without going into the details, the result is a slight (typically, 10 to 15 per cent) increase in data transfer speed.

This provides a way of reducing the traditional performance bottleneck caused by memory not being able to run at the same speed as the CPU.

64-Bit Motherboards

These boards are designed for 64-bit CPUs, which can process 64 bits of data simultaneously as opposed to the 32 bit capabilities of standard CPUs. As a result, performance is enhanced considerably.

However, you should be aware that current 32-bit software is not able to fully utilize the benefits offered by a 64-bit system. To do so requires a 64-bit operating system, programs and hardware drivers. At the time of writing, 64-bit versions of Windows, Linux and Mac OS X are available, but 64-bit applications and hardware drivers are very thin on the ground.

By all means buy a 64-bit system; it will run all your existing software with a degree of improvement. This will be an upgrade for the future though, as it is going to be a while before mainstream software is available in 64-bit versions.

Hot tip

All the setups described on this page are intended for those who require high levels of performance.

Hot tip

64-bit architecture is the direction in which the computer world is heading. While it is going to be a while before it becomes mainstream, it is going to happen.

Installing a Motherboard

1 Strip the existing board and disconnect all the cables

2 Unscrew the board

3 Remove it from the case

Don't forget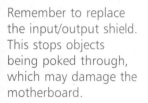

Remember to replace the input/output shield. This stops objects being poked through, which may damage the motherboard.

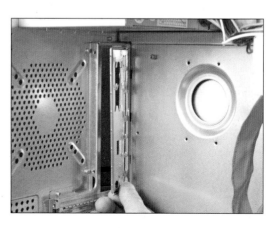

4 Remove the input/output panel shield then fit the new one

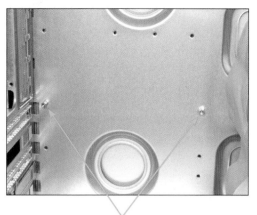

5 Hold the new board against the brass standoffs to make sure they align with the screw holes. If not, relocate them as necessary

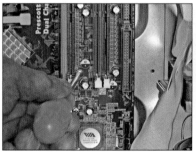

6 Screw the new board down

7 Reconnect your devices

8 Reconnect the cables for the case switches, speaker, and LEDs

Configuring the BIOS

When the system is back in one piece, certain configuration settings in the BIOS need to be changed. This is done via the BIOS setup program, which is accessed by pressing a key as the PC boots (the key will be specified at the bottom of the first boot screen), as shown below:

```
Phoenix — AwardBIOS v6.00PC, An Energy Star Ally
Copyright © 1984–2003, Phoenix Technologies, Ltd

KM266M.B12 For KM266-MNB

Main Processor : AMD Athlon 1200Mhz
Memory Testing : 262144K OK

    Primary Master  : ST340014A 3.54
     Primary Slave  : None
  Secondary Master  : LITE-ON LTR-52327S QSOB
   Secondary Slave  : None




Press Del to enter SETUP
10/09/2003-KM266-8235-6A6LVP8CC-00
```

BIOS setup program entry key

Navigating the BIOS is done using the following keys:

- Up arrow key – moves the cursor up

- Down arrow key – moves the cursor down

- Left arrow key – moves the cursor left

- Right arrow key – moves the cursor right

- Page Up key – selects a higher value

- Page Down key – selects a lower value

- Enter key – make a selection

- Escape key – return to the previous menu

Date and Time

The first setting that must be changed is the date and time (assuming it hasn't already been set by the motherboard manufacturer). Do this as follows:

1 On the BIOS main page, select Standard CMOS Features using the arrow keys

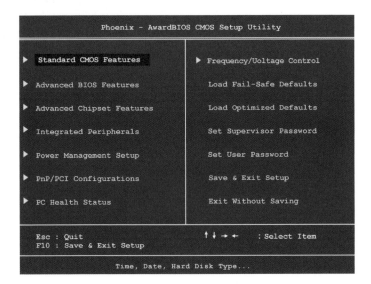

1 Scroll to Date, and Time, respectively, and enter the correct figures using the Page Up/Page Down keys

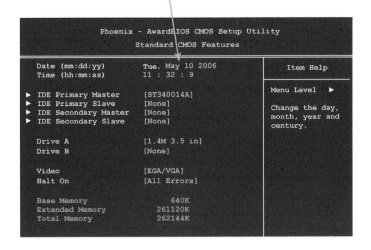

...cont'd

Floppy Drive

We're assuming here that your system has one of these devices; not all do these days. Open the Standard CMOS Features page as described on the previous page.

Those of you with an AMI BIOS will find the floppy drive configuration setting on the Advanced Page.

1 Scroll down to "None", opposite Drive A

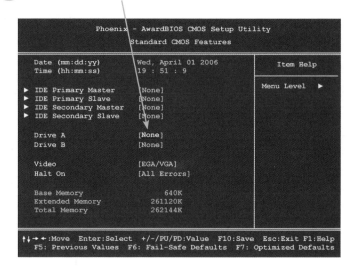

Hot tip

Some BIOS programs automatically detect and configure the floppy drive. Not all do though, in which case you should follow the procedure detailed on this page.

2 Using the Page Up/Page Down keys, select the "1.44M 3.5 in" option. The system will now recognize the floppy drive

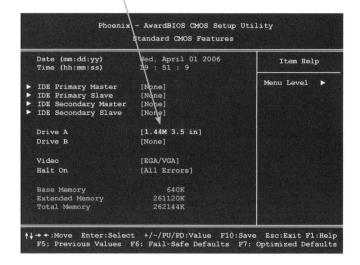

USB

In many BIOSs, the USB bus is disabled by default. Enable it as follows:

1 On the main BIOS page, select Integrated Peripherals. Then scroll down to Onchip PCI Device

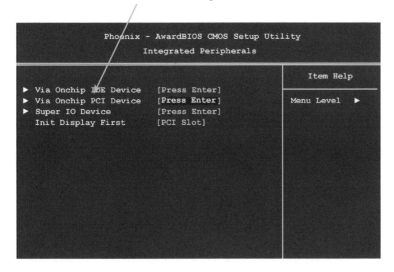

2 Press Enter to open the Onchip PCI Device page, scroll to Onchip USB Controller and set it to Enabled

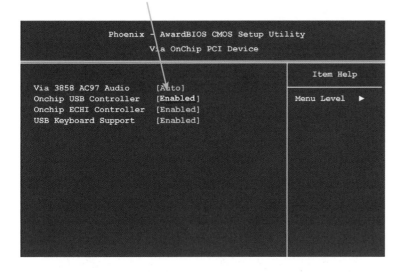

Hot tip

The USB setting in AMI BIOSs is on the Advanced page.

Hot tip

When you have finished setting up the BIOS, the changes must be saved before you exit the program. Otherwise, they will revert back to the original settings. Do this by going to the main page and selecting Save and Exit Setup. Press Enter and then Y to confirm.

Hot tip

Note that if you are using an AGP video card, this may also have to be set up in the BIOS. See pages 173-174 for details of how to do this.

Also, if your system has a sound card, the motherboard's integrated sound system will have to be disabled. See page 176.

Upgrading the BIOS

The BIOS is responsible for initializing the PC's bootup procedure, and recognizing and configuring the system's hardware prior to the loading of the operating system.

Like every other part of the computer, the development of new technology renders the BIOS program out-of-date. Fortunately, modern BIOSs can be upgraded by means of a flash utility (see margin note).

But how do you know when your BIOS needs upgrading? The answer is when you need to run software or a hardware device that uses technology not supported by the BIOS. This can be established by reading the relevant documentation. The following are typical examples:

- CPU support – the BIOS enables the motherboard to accept CPUs up to a certain speed, or of a certain type. In many cases, older motherboards can be made compatible with more recent CPUs by a BIOS upgrade

- Large hard drive support – due to inherent limitations, older BIOSs will recognize only part of a hard drive's total capacity. For example, many older BIOSs cannot recognize more than 137.4 GB. So a user buying a 200 GB drive may have the frustration of being unable to use a third of it. One solution to this problem is to upgrade the BIOS

- Bug fixes – all software contains errors; BIOS programs are no different. By making upgrades available, manufacturers are able to offer fixes

Performing a BIOS Upgrade

Having decided that there is a need to upgrade the BIOS, proceed as follows:

1) The first step is to correctly identify the model number of both the motherboard and the BIOS chip

Hot tip

Modern BIOSs are flash upgradable, which means that the instructions they contain can be overwritten with updated versions. To do it, you need the update file, which is available from the motherboard's manufacturer, and a flash utility.

Note that many older BIOSs are not upgradable.

Beware

The most critical part of BIOS upgrading is getting the correct update file. To this end, you must be able to correctly identify the manufacturer and model number of both the BIOS and the motherboard.

2)   Locate and obtain the BIOS update file. This will be available at the motherboard manufacturer's website. You will also need an upgrading utility. These are known as "flash" utilities and will also be available from the motherboard manufacturer (see margin note)

3)   Double-click the downloaded BIOS file (this is usually in a zipped format) and extract the contents to a blank formatted floppy disk. If a flash utility isn't included, you'll have to copy one to the floppy disk as well

4)   Now create a boot floppy disk. See page 166 for instructions on how to do this

5)   Place the boot floppy disk in the floppy drive and reboot the PC. When the PC has booted up, replace the boot disk with the one containing the BIOS file and the flash utility. From this point on, you will have to follow the instructions included with the flash utility as the procedure varies according to the utility used. Typically though, it involves little more than simply typing in the name of the update file and its location, and then pressing Enter

A typical BIOS flash utility

Upgrading System Buses

A PC's bus is a communication channel that passes data to and from its components. Think of it as a road system with the individual components all having their own address on the road and you'll get the picture.

Different parts of the system use different types of bus, e.g. the front side bus for data transfer between the motherboard, the CPU and memory, the ATA/SATA buses for the system's drives, the AGP/PCI Express x16 buses for video, etc.

As computer technology advances, buses (and hence the devices that use them) become obsolete and are replaced with new ones. Thus, upgraders may find that their system is not compatible with the bus used by modern devices. Some of these buses, such as the motherboard's FSB, cannot be upgraded without replacing the motherboard.

However, there are some that can. These are the ones that are used to connect external devices, such as printers, scanners, Rev drives, etc. Drive buses can be upgraded as well.

All that's necessary is to buy a PCI card that contains the appropriate bus technology and ports, and connect it to a PCI socket on the motherboard.

Here we have a PCI card that provides two USB 2 ports, and also two FireWire ports

This card adds the SATA drive interface to the system

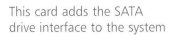

5 Store More On Your PC

In this chapter, we look at the PC's main data storage device – the hard drive. You'll learn about the various interfaces used by these devices and important specifications – factors that need to be considered when buying a drive.

Hard Drives

Hard drives are one of the components most likely to fail in a computer system. This is because they are mechanical devices that use motors, bearings and other moving parts. Inevitably, these parts are subject to wear and tear and will eventually fail. When a hard drive does fail, it is almost always terminal – these devices cannot usually be repaired. Any data that was on the drive will be lost.

Unfortunately, they also happen to be one of the more difficult components to upgrade. The physical installation is easy enough (just four screws and two cables – interface and power). What's not quite so straightforward is the configuration of these devices and preparing them for use (partitioning and formatting).

Furthermore, if the drive being replaced is the main system drive on which is loaded the operating system, then this will have to re-installed, plus any programs installed on it.

Yet another complication is choosing the best type of drive for your purposes, e.g. SCSI, SATA, ATA, etc

The following pages explain everything you need to know to carry out a hard drive upgrade successfully.

Does it Need Upgrading?

There are three reasons to upgrade a hard drive:

1) The existing drive has failed, or is beginning to fail
2) To take advantage of more recent drive technology
3) More storage capacity is needed

In the first two instances, there is nothing to think about – the drive has to be replaced. In the latter case, however, an upgrade may not be necessary.

If you've been using your drive for some time and have now run out of space, it could be time to simply have a clear-out and get rid of redundant data. The quickest and easiest way to do this is as follows:

1 Go to Start, All Programs, Accessories, System Tools, and Disk Cleanup

2 Select the drive to be cleaned up. After a few moments, you will be presented with a list of files that can be safely deleted. Make your selection by checking the appropriate boxes and click OK

Clicking the More Options tab gives you three more options:

1) The removal of Windows components that are not used
2) The removal of third-party programs that are not used
3) The deletion of System Restore files (see margin note)

Work through these and delete as much stuff as you can.

Beware

The following are all signs of a hard drive that's on the way out, and need to be acted upon if you don't want to lose all your data:

• Unusual levels of mechanical noise

• The PC locks-up frequently

• File system errors (indicated by Chkdsk)

• Spurious loss of data

Hot tip

Those of you running versions of Windows from Me onwards have a utility known as System Restore. This is used to restore the system to a previous state in the event of problems, and it works by taking a snapshot of the system at periodic intervals and saving it as a file. These files can be huge, and a number of them can occupy several gigabytes of hard drive space.

...cont'd

This should free up enough hard drive space to cover most purposes, particularly if you had a lot of System Restore files.

Fragmentation

Another issue that must be considered is that of fragmentation. This is a process in which files saved to a drive are split up, i.e. fragmented, into smaller pieces and saved on different locations on the drive. This means that the drive's read/write heads have to hunt about for a file's fragments and re-assemble them into the complete file before presenting it to the user.

This is a time consuming process, the effect of which is that the file takes a lot longer to open. To the user, it seems that the system is running slowly and he/she may conclude that the CPU and/or memory (or even the hard drive itself) needs upgrading, when in reality all that's required is simple maintenance.

So before upgrading any component in an attempt to improve the performance of your system, try defragmenting the hard drive first. This procedure reverses the fragmentation process and will give the system a considerable boost. Do it as follows:

 Users of Windows versions prior to Vista (if you are using Vista see bottom margin note) should go to: Start, All Programs, Accessories, System Tools and Disk Defragmenter. Select Drive C and click Defragment

Hot tip

Vista users have no need to concern themselves about drive fragmentation – the defragmentation utility is enabled by default and works in the background without any need for input by the user.

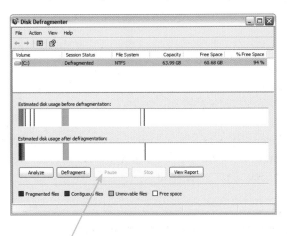

The defragmentation procedure in process. Note that this can take a long time to complete

Internal Hard Drives

Having made the decision to upgrade your hard drive, your next decision is what type of drive to go for. These devices are classified by the interface used, e.g. a SATA drive runs from the SATA interface.

Internal hard drives use one of three interfaces: ATA, SATA or SCSI. External models, which we look at on page 73, use either the USB 2, FireWire or E-SATA interface.

ATA

The ATA (Advanced Technology Attachment) standard originated way back in 1986 and has since undergone many evolutions, which have increased the speed and size of the drives that it can support. The current one is ATA-8, which supports data transfer speeds of up to 133 MB/s. However, due to the introduction of the SATA interface (below), this is likely to be the last update for ATA. In other words, it is now on the way out.

SATA

SATA (Serial ATA) is a development of the ATA interface and provides several major improvements. These include:

- Data transfer speeds – the first generation of SATA, SATA 1, had a data transfer speed of 150 MB/s, compared with a maximum of 133 MB/s for ATA. The current SATA generation (SATA 2) transfers data at 300 MB/s, and future generations are expected to offer at least 600 MB/s

- Hot-swapping capabilities – SATA drives can be connected and disconnected while the PC is running, unlike ATA drives, which require the PC to be powered off before this can be done

- Power requirements – SATA drives have a lower power requirement than ATA drives, which in turn means that less heat is generated

- Improved airflow – SATA drives use a slimline interface cable that offers less resistance to airflow than the 80-wire ribbon cables used by ATA drives

Hot tip

The ATA interface can be confusing for the uninitiated as it goes by several names. When you see a drive described by any of the following, it is an ATA drive:

- IDE
- EIDE
- DMA
- UDMA
- PATA
- ATA

Hot tip

Unlike ATA, where two separate drives can be connected to a single socket, SATA allows only one.

- Setting up – SATA drives do not need to be configured as master or slave as do ATA drives (see page 77)

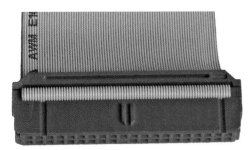

SATA cable   ATA ribbon cable

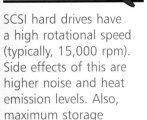

Hot tip

SCSI hard drives have a high rotational speed (typically, 15,000 rpm). Side effects of this are higher noise and heat emission levels. Also, maximum storage capacities are less than with ATA and SATA drives.

E-SATA

E-SATA is a development of the SATA interface and is intended for use with external drives. Its advantage is that it allows data transfer to take place at the same speed as internal SATA drives (USB 2 and FireWire external drives are considerably slower than internal ATA drives).

SCSI

SCSI (Small Computer System Interface) is actually a system interface that can be used with any type of SCSI device – it is not restricted for use with hard drives.

SCSI hard drives provide fast data transfer speeds (320 MB/s), high levels of performance and are extremely reliable. These qualities make them ideal for use in server and corporate environments, which is in fact, where they are normally seen.

Don't forget

If you wish to take advantage of the high performance levels and reliability offered by SCSI hard drives, you will need to add the SCSI interface to your system.

They do have some disadvantages, though. Firstly, they are very expensive (costing, typically, four times as much as an ATA/SATA drive of similar capacity).

Secondly, as very few motherboards have native support for SCSI, it is usually necessary to install a SCSI adaptor card. This adds further to the expense. However, once fitted, the adaptor card allows you to run other SCSI devices as well, thus increasing the system's expansion options.

External Hard Drives

External hard drives use one of 3 interfaces: USB 2, FireWire or E-SATA. E-SATA is the fastest (twice as fast as FireWire 800 and 6 times as fast as USB 2) and is thus the recommended option.

One of the main benefits of these devices is ease of installation; simply plug them in and they are ready to go. Unlike internal models, they are supplied pre-partitioned and formatted, and do not require jumper configuration (see page 77).

One of the main benefits of these devices is ease of installation; simply plug them in and they are ready to go. Unlike internal models, they are supplied pre-partitioned and formatted, and do not require jumper configuration (see page 77).

Hot tip

For those of you who like to keep things simple, an external hard drive is the way to go.

Other advantages include:

- Easy transportation of data – simply unplug from one PC and connect to another

- Higher capacities – internal drives are limited in terms of physical size by the constraints of the system case, which in turn limits their maximum storage capacity (currently 1 TB). External models have no such limits

However, they do have some disadvantages and these are:

- Because they have to be supplied in a robust case and sometimes with a separate power supply, they cost much more than internal models of equivalent capacity

- They cannot be used as the main system drive, i.e. you can't install the operating system on them. Thus, they are restricted to additional storage purposes

- Data transfer speed – external drives using the USB and FireWire interfaces are slower than internal drives. However, E-SATA models are as fast as internal drives

Beware

External hard drives are much more expensive than internal drives.

Hard Drive Capacity Limitations

Users with an old PC need to be aware of a problem that is caused by older BIOS chips – your system may not recognize the full capacity of a modern hard drive. This is due to limitations inherent in the BIOS and, in some cases, the operating system.

We won't go into the reasons for this but it comes down to the fact that when the ATA drive interface was developed, the design of hard drives did not take into account the amazing increase in drive storage capacity that was to follow. As the various limitations became apparent (528 MB, 2.1 GB, 4.2 GB, 8.4 GB, 32 GB and 137 GB), various methods of overcoming them were developed.

The easiest and most commonly used of these is the Dynamic Disk Overlay (DDO) method. Basically, this overrides the part of the BIOS instructions that address the issue of hard drive translation, and thus enables the full capacity of a drive to be recognized. A DDO program is usually provided by hard drive manufacturers (assuming you buy a retail version – if you buy an OEM version, you will have to download the program from the manufacturer's website). However, there are issues with DDO (see margin note) that make it a less than ideal method.

A much better way is to flash upgrade the BIOS (see pages 64-65). This provides a permanent solution that has no software ramifications (as does the DDO method). However, the BIOS chips on really old systems cannot be upgraded, in which case, DDO provides the only realistic solution.

The latest drive capacity limitation is 137 GB. To overcome this requires not only the BIOS issue to be addressed, but also that the operating system is able to support 48-bit hard drive addressing. The solution is as follows:

- Windows Vista – has native support for 48-bit hard drive addressing, so no action is necessary

- Windows XP – install Service Pack 2

- Windows 2000 – install Service Pack 3

- Windows 95sr2/98/Me/NT – install a 48-bit controller card

Beware

The DDO method of overcoming BIOS hard drive limitations is not as good as upgrading the BIOS and can be the cause of several problems. These include:

- Operating system issues – the installation of a new operating system, or setting up of a dual-boot system can cause bootup and data loss problems

- DDO can be very difficult to remove from a system and may require the use of a special program

- Compatibility issues – if you have two hard drives in your system, each from a different manufacturer, you may have problems getting both to work

Having said all this, if you don't do anything out of the ordinary with your PC, DDO will be OK.

Hard Drive Specifications

It is essential that you buy a good quality hard drive and to ensure that you do, look at the relevant specifications. The best place to find these is the manufacturer's, or seller's, website. A typical example is shown below:

Specifications	
Capacity	80 GB
External Data Transfer Rate	150 MBps
Internal Data Transfer Rate	760 Mbit/s
Seek Time	8 ms
Buffer Size	8 MB
Interface	Serial ATA
Rotational Speed	7200 rpm

Looking at these from the top, we have:

Capacity

Hard drive capacity is measured in gigabytes (GB) and is the specification (often, the only specification) most commonly looked at by buyers. We cannot tell you what you need in this respect – it depends entirely on what you use the PC for. However, when making your decision, bear the following in mind:

- Consider your future requirements as well. Whereas, years ago, lack of hard drive capacity was a limiting factor in software design, this is no longer the case and software applications can now be enormous in size

- Hard drives do not perform at their best when they are at, or close to, maximum capacity – data transfer rates drop. As a rough guide, twenty per cent of their capacity should be unused in order to achieve maximum performance

External Data Transfer Rate

This is the speed at which data is transferred from the drive to the system, and vice versa. The difference between the various versions of ATA (100 to 133 MB/s) and SATA 1 (150 MB/s) is marginal and really isn't an issue.

...cont'd

Hot tip

Currently, SATA 2 provides the fastest data transfer speed for internal drives. For external drives, E-SATA is the fastest.

Hot tip

Some manufacturers specify a drive's Seek Time and others specify Access Time. Whichever, a figure of around 8 Ms is good.

Hot tip

Look for a rotational speed of 7200 rpm. Cheaper drives will have one of 5400. SCSI drives offer rotational speeds between 10,000 and 15,000.

However, the difference between ATA/SATA 1, and SATA 2 (300 MB/s) and SCSI (320 MB/s) is considerable.

Internal Data Transfer Rate

This is the speed at which a drive can write and read data to and from its disks and is a very important indication of its performance.

Seek/Access Time

This is a measure of the time required for the drive's read/write heads to move between tracks over the surfaces of the disks. Note that Seek Time and Access Time are actually different specs but are close enough to be considered the same.

Rotational Speed

This is a measure of how fast a drive's disk platters spin and is a very important specification, as it directly affects the speed at which the drive reads and writes data. The faster the rotational speed the better the drive's performance.

Buffer Size

The buffer is an area of high-speed memory that is used to store frequently accessed data in order to improve performance. The size is not critical (2 MB is adequate for most users). Power-users, however, will benefit from a higher buffer size.

The following table sums up typical specifications for hard drives aimed at different sections of the market.

	Low-End	Mid-Range	High-End
Drive Type	ATA	SATA 1	SATA 2/SCSI
External Data Transfer Rate	100/133	150	300 - 320
Internal Data Transfer Rate	400-600	600-750	800-900
Seek/Access Time	12	8.5	3.6
Rotational Speed	5400	7200	7200-15,000
Buffer Size	2	2	8

Configuring an ATA Hard Drive

The ATA interface can handle two drives simultaneously. For this reason, an order of preference must be set in which one drive is the master and the other the slave.

To facilitate this, ATA hard drives are supplied with a jumper block at the rear, which has four pairs of pins, each pair providing a different configuration. A 2-pin jumper is used to select the one required.

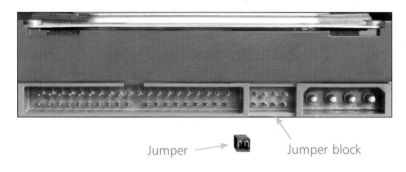

Jumper →   Jumper block

Hot tip

A drive that is configured as the master will provide better performance as it is connected directly to the system. The slave is connected via the master.

Hot tip

The SATA interface can handle only one drive, so no configuration is necessary. However, SATA motherboards provide at least two of these interfaces, so you can still use two drives.

77

If you are just replacing the existing drive, all you have to do is confirm that the jumper is in the correct position to set the drive as the master. While most drives are supplied with this as the default setting, you have to check (the jumper could have worked loose during transit, for example).

To enable users to place the jumpers correctly, most drives have a jumper setting table printed on the case, as shown right.

If you are installing a second drive, the drive on which the operating system is installed should be set as the master; this will give the best results. Also, it should be the faster or newer of the two.

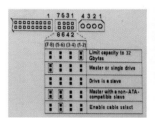

Installing an ATA Hard Drive

Beware

Hard drives are delicate devices and do not respond well to knocks and being dropped.

 Move the floppy drive cable out of the way

2 Slide the drive into position

Beware

If you fit the drive upside down, it won't work for long. The 4-pin power socket should be on the right.

3 Secure the drive with the supplied screws

Hot tip

80-pin ATA interface cables are keyed to make sure they are fitted the right way round. If the plug won't fit one way, try the other.

4 Connect the black end of the drive interface cable to the ATA socket

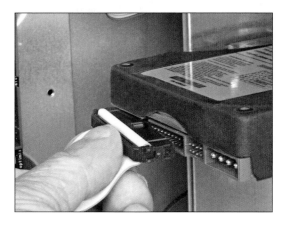

5 Connect the power supply

6 Locate the colored ATA socket on the motherboard

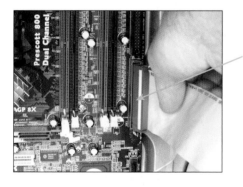

7 Connect the other end of the interface cable (with the colored plug) to the motherboard

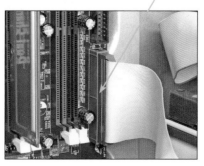

Installing a Second ATA Hard Drive

Leaving a space between hard drives prevents heat from one affecting the other. It's not critical but if the space is there it is good practice to use it.

Don't forget

The slave connector is in the middle of the interface cable, as shown below.

1 Slide the drive into the next but one bay from the main drive (see top margin note)

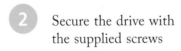

80

Don't forget

Remember to configure the drive as the slave by means of the appropriate jumper setting.

2 Secure the drive with the supplied screws

3 Connect the gray slave interface plug to the drive

4 Connect a power plug

Installing a SATA Hard Drive

This is exactly the same procedure as for an ATA drive. The only difference is that SATA drives use a different type of cable and require a driver if Windows XP is the operating system

 Connect one end of the power cable to the socket at the left of the drive

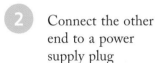 Connect the other end to a power supply plug

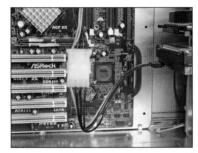

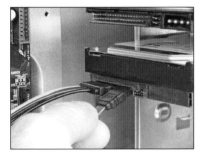

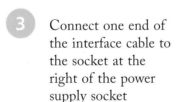 Connect one end of the interface cable to the socket at the right of the power supply socket

Connect the other end to the SATA 1 socket on the motherboard. This is for the primary drive (the SATA 2 socket is for a second SATA drive)

Hot tip

If you wish to do so, you can have both ATA and SATA drives connected to the system.

Hot tip

If the SATA drive is intended to be the boot drive and the operating system is Windows XP, you will have to do the following:

• Copy the SATA driver to a floppy disk (if it isn't already supplied on one by the motherboard manufacturer). Instructions for this will be in the motherboard manual

• Install the drive

• Start the XP installation

• When prompted, press F6 to install RAID or SCSI drivers

• When prompted for the driver, place the floppy disk in the drive, select the driver and press Enter

Note that Windows Vista provides native support for SATA and so does not require the above procedure.

RAID Configurations

For those of you who have two or more hard drives in your system, there is another configuration option. This is known as

RAID (Redundant Array of Independent Disks), and it is a method of configuring a combination of hard drives so as to gain specific benefits, such as data protection and increased performance.

This type of configuration is set up after the drives have been installed and requires either a hardware RAID controller, or a RAID software program. Virtually all current motherboards provide a controller.

The various RAID configurations are:

RAID 0

This requires a minimum of two drives, and works by splitting (known as striping) the data equally between them. The result is much improved data transfer speeds as each drive handles part of a file.

RAID 1

This also requires a minimum of two drives. In this configuration, all data saved is duplicated (known as mirroring) on each drive. The purpose is data protection – if one drive fails, the data is recoverable from the other/s.

RAID 0+1

This is a combination of RAID 0 and RAID 1 and requires a minimum of four drives. Half the drives are used to stripe the data, and the other half to mirror it. Thus, it provides fast data transfer, together with data protection.

RAID 5

This requires a minimum of three drives. Data is striped across all the drives, but an error checking bit (known as the parity bit), is also stored. Should any one drive fail, the RAID controller will calculate the missing data and keep the system running until the faulty drive can be replaced.

Beware

Software RAID controllers place a heavy load on the operating system, and thus have an adverse effect on overall system performance. Nor are they as reliable or efficient as hardware controllers.

82

Hot tip

RAID setups are expensive and are most commonly found in server and corporate environments. Unless you have a need for extreme levels of performance or data protection, they really aren't necessary.

Partitioning and Formatting

An internal hard drive must be partitioned before it can be used. If this is not done, the drive won't be recognized by the system, i.e. if you go to My Computer, it won't be there.

When the partition has been created, it must then be formatted. This process organizes it into logical units known as blocks, sectors and tracks. These are used by the operating system to "remember" where specific data is stored on the drive.

The procedures vary according to which version of Windows you are using (we are going to look at Windows XP and Windows Vista here), and also on whether the drive is to be used purely for extra storage or is going to be the main system drive, i.e. where Windows is installed.

Drive to be Used as Extra Storage

This is the more straightforward of the two scenarios as the procedures can be done within Windows. The following applies to both XP and Vista.

1 Go to Start, Control Panel, Administrative Tools

2 Click Computer Management and then on the left-hand side, click Disk Management

3 After a few moments, the following window will appear (taken from Vista)

Hot tip

Drives can be split into a number of partitions, each of which appear to the operating system as a separate hard drive. Alternatively, one partition equal to the entire capacity of the drive can be created (this is the usual setup).

83

...cont'd

This shows all the hard drives in the system.

4   Right-click the drive to be partitioned (Disk 0 in the screenshot on page 83) and click New Simple Volume (volume is Microsoft parlance for a partition). Windows New Simple Volume Wizard will open. Click Next

5   Click Next in the two dialog boxes that follow

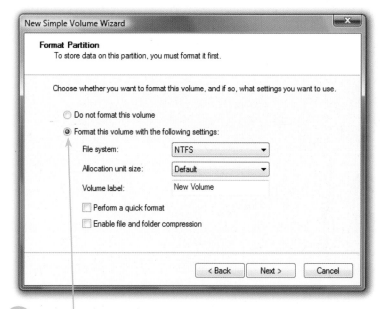

6   Select "Format this volume..." and click Next. Windows will now partition and format the drive. When the procedure is complete, the drive will be available for use

System Drive

When Windows is going to be installed on the drive, fairly obviously, the partitioning and formatting procedures cannot be done within Windows. In this case, they have to be done from the installation disk.

Installing Windows Vista on the System Drive

The first thing to do is set the system to boot from the CD/DVD drive. Do this as follows:

1 Restart the PC and enter the BIOS setup program as described previously

2 On the main page, select Advanced BIOS Features and press Enter

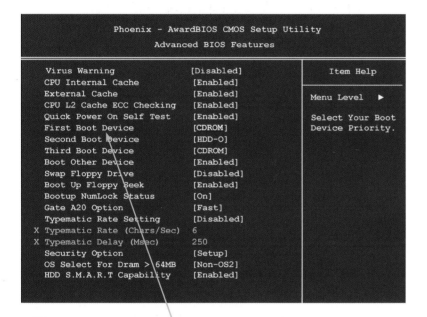

```
            Phoenix - AwardBIOS CMOS Setup Utility
                    Advanced BIOS Features

   Virus Warning               [Disabled]          Item Help
   CPU Internal Cache          [Enabled]
   External Cache              [Enabled]        Menu Level    ▶
   CPU L2 Cache ECC Checking   [Enabled]
   Quick Power On Self Test    [Enabled]        Select Your Boot
   First Boot Device           [CDROM]          Device Priority.
   Second Boot Device          [HDD-O]
   Third Boot Device           [CDROM]
   Boot Other Device           [Enabled]
   Swap Floppy Drive           [Disabled]
   Boot Up Floppy Seek         [Enabled]
   Bootup NumLock Status       [On]
   Gate A20 Option             [Fast]
   Typematic Rate Setting      [Disabled]
 X Typematic Rate (Chars/Sec)  6
 X Typematic Delay (Msec)      250
   Security Option             [Setup]
   OS Select For Dram >\64MB   [Non-OS2]
   HDD S.M.A.R.T Capability    [Enabled]
```

3 Scroll down to First Boot Device, and using the Page Up/Page Down keys, select CDROM. Save the change and exit the BIOS

With the CD/DVD drive configured as the first boot device, insert Vista's installation disk into the drive and boot the PC. When the second boot screen flashes up, you'll see a message that says "Press any key to boot from CD...". Do so and Vista will begin loading its installation files to the hard drive.

Don't forget

Note that you should restore the boot order to its original setting when the partitioning and formatting procedure is complete. In case you forget, the first boot device should be the floppy drive, followed by the hard drive and CD-ROM drive respectively.

Don't forget

To use Vista's partitioning and formatting tools, the CD/DVD drive must be set as the first boot device. Otherwise, they won't be accessible.

1 At the first screen, click Install now

2 At the second screen, select your preferences – installation language, time and currency format, and keyboard layout

3 Enter the product key and OK the license agreement. Then at the "Which type of installation do you want?" screen, select Custom (advanced)

4 At the next screen, "Where do you want to install Windows?", click Drive Options (advanced)

5 Click New

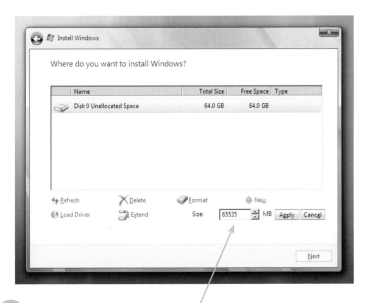

By default, Vista will select the largest possible partition size (equal to the size of the hard drive).

6 Enter the required partition size (see margin note) and click Apply. Then click Next

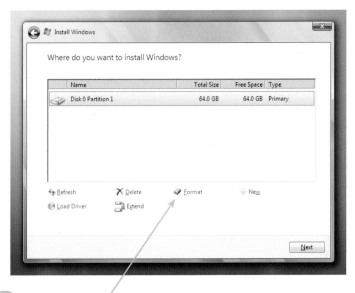

7 Click Format. When the format procedure has finished, Vista's setup routine will begin automatically

...cont'd

Installing Windows XP on the System Drive

As with Vista, Windows XP has be installed from the installation disk, which means that the system must be set to boot from the CD/DVD drive as described on page 85. Then restart the PC with the installation disk inserted and the installation files will be copied to the hard drive.

1 The first screen will be Welcome to Setup. Press Enter

Beware

The "Press any key to boot from CD..." message is displayed only for a few seconds. If you miss it, press the reset button and try again.

2 The second screen will be the license agreement. OK this and press Enter

3 Next, you'll see the installation options screen, as shown below

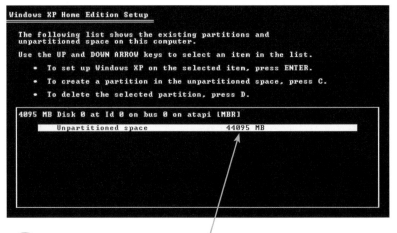

4 In the box, you will see the total size of the drive next to "Unpartitioned space". By pressing Enter, XP will create a single partition equal to this size

5 Should you wish to create two or more partitions, press
C at step 4. The screen that opens allows you to select the
number and size of the partitions you want

```
Windows XP Home Edition Setup

  You asked Setup to create a new partition on
  4095 MB Disk 0 at Id 0 on bus 0 on atapi [MBR].

    • To create the new partition, enter a size below and
      press ENTER.

    • To go back to the previous screen without creating
      the partition, press ESC.

  The minimum size for the new partition is     8 megabytes (MB).
  The maximum size for the new partition is  4087 megabytes (MB).
  Create partition of size (in MB):  4087
```

For the purpose of this tutorial, however, we will assume that you
want a single partition, so just press Enter at step 4. The partition
will be created and you will then be taken to the format screen, as
shown below

```
Windows XP Home Edition Setup

  A new partition for Windows XP has been created on

  4095 MB Disk 0 at Id 0 on bus 0 on atapi [MBR].

  This partition must now be formatted.

  From the list below, select a file system for the new partition.
  Use the UP and DOWN ARROW keys to select the file system you want,
  and then press ENTER.

  If you want to select a different partition for Windows XP,
  press ESC.

    Format the partition using the NTFS file system (Quick)
    Format the partition using the FAT file system (Quick)
    Format the partition using the NTFS file system
    Format the partition using the FAT file system
```

6 Select "Format the partition using the NTFS file system"
and press Enter. Now all you have to do is sit back as
Windows XP installs itself

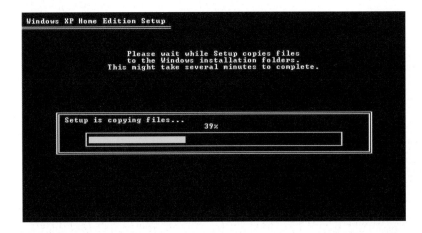

Hot tip

The time taken for the Windows installation to complete depends on the specifications of your computer.

90

Simply follow the prompts and within twenty minutes or so, the installation will be complete.

6 Removable Media Options

This chapter looks at drives that provide a more permanent, and thus reliable means of data storage than offered by hard drives.

Floppy Drives – Are They Worth It?

While these devices are painfully slow and the disks hold a pitiful amount of data (1.44 MB) by today's standards, they are, nevertheless, still useful in many ways. Some typical applications are: small hardware drivers (mice, keyboards, etc), BIOS flash upgrades, rescue disks, and text documents (a floppy disk will hold a full length novel).

So a floppy drive that has failed is usually worth replacing, particularly as they cost only a few dollars. Is it worth replacing a good one with a more recent model, though? Will there be any performance gains? The short answer to this is no, as the basic technology behind them hasn't changed for years. A drive bought today will be no faster than one bought ten years ago.

However, some of today's floppy drives do come with an additional feature that will be useful to many users.

This is a built-in flash card reader. Apart from handling floppy disks, these drives can also read, and transfer to the hard drive, the contents of various types of flash memory. For example: Compact Flash, MicroDrive, MemoryStick, SmartMedia, MultiMedia and Secure Digital Cards.

Also available is an advanced type of floppy drive known as a Superdisk drive. These devices have exactly the same dimensions as a standard floppy drive and are compatible with 1.44 MB floppy disks. However, they can also be used with a different type of disk (superdisk) that has capacities of up to 250 MB. Furthermore, they incorporate a formatting technology that increases the capacity of a floppy disk to a comparatively massive 32 MB.

So if you have a need for any of these features, a floppy drive upgrade can be worth while.

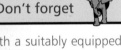
Don't forget

With a suitably equipped floppy drive, you can look at the pictures on your digicam directly from the memory card.

Installing a Floppy Drive

Hot tip

The floppy drive bay is at the top of the lower 3.5 inch drive cage.

1 Slide the drive into the top of the 3.5 inch drive cage (above the hard drive). You can do this from the rear or from the front

2 Secure the drive

Hot tip

Power is supplied to the floppy drive via the 4-pin connector, as shown below.

3 Connect the power supply

...cont'd

Hot tip

The red stripe corresponds to pin 1 on both the motherboard and drive sockets.

Unlike those for hard drives, floppy drive interface connectors are not keyed at the drive end. This makes it possible to fit them the wrong way round. To make sure that you don't do this, the cable has a red stripe along one side and also a twist at one end, as shown left. The twisted end connects to the drive, with the stripe on the left-hand side, as shown below.

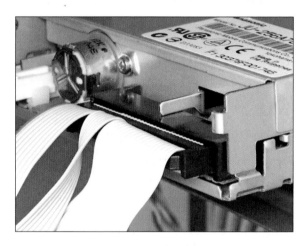

4 Red stripe on the left, twisted end to the drive

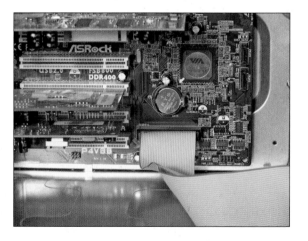

5 The motherboard connector is keyed, so it will only fit one way (red stripe on the left)

CD-ROM Drives

A CD-ROM drive can read the data on a CD but no more than that; it cannot write data. For this reason, these devices are one of the most commonly upgraded parts of a PC, as writing capability is an essential function for many people these days.

When considering a replacement, the upgrader has a number of options from which to choose:

1) Firstly, a like-for-like swap can be made, i.e. a CD-ROM drive for a CD-ROM drive. This is rather pointless though, as explained in option 2 below

2) The CD-ROM drive can be replaced with a CD writer. These devices are able to write to a CD, as well as read from them

3) The upgrader also has two DVD options. The first is a DVD-ROM drive, which, as with the CD-ROM drive, is only able to read discs. However, they are able to read CDs as well as DVDs. The second is a DVD writer, which as well as being able to read DVDs and CDs, can also write to DVD and CD discs

4) Now available (if your pocket can stand the strain) are Blu-Ray and HD-DVD drives

CD Writers

When these drives were first introduced, the discs they used were only capable of being written to once (CD-R). It wasn't long though, before re-writable models (CD-RW), which could erase the contents of a disc and reuse it, hit the market. These required a disc of a different composition that allowed rewriting.

CD rewriters (CD-RW) are now the minimum in new PCs (most now provide a DVD rewriter). The older CD writers (CD-R) have been phased out. So when you come to upgrade your old CD-ROM drive, a CD-RW is the minimum you should go for.

Even if you presently have no need for disc writing, this is a feature that you will undoubtedly find a use for in the future. In the meantime, it will read your CDs. When you do upgrade it will be useful to know the pros and cons of the two types of recordable disc.

CD-R

This is the most commonly used type of writable disc. They are cheap, the writing process is quicker than it is with CD-RW, and they have a longer expected shelf-life than CD-RWs. They are also considered to be more reliable, i.e. there is less chance of data corruption.

CD-RW

The big advantage of these discs (indeed, the only advantage) is that they can be reused – if you believe what the manufacturers say – about a thousand times.

So unless you do a lot of non-permanent disc writing, the advice is to stick with your CD-R drive.

DVD Writers

DVD (Digital Versatile Disc) is an optical data technology that provides extremely high storage capacities. A standard DVD can hold 4.7 GB of data, and a dual-layer DVD (which has two data layers) can hold 8.5 GB.

For this reason, DVD discs are used for commercially produced movies, as an entire movie can be fitted on one disc. These seriously high levels of storage capacity are also being utilized by the PC industry.

For example, Microsoft's Encarta Reference Library, which requires five CDs is available on a single DVD. With the ever increasing size of software applications, you can expect to see many more of them shipped on DVD discs in the near future. This is one reason to buy a DVD drive.

The high capacity of DVD discs is handy for PC users as well. Typical applications are large-scale system backups, storage of high-resolution video and TV shows recorded via TV tuner devices.

Hot tip

CD-R discs are the best choice for virtually all purposes. They are cheaper, quicker in operation and offer more reliable storage than CD-RW discs. Another advantage is that they are more compatible with home and car CD players.

Another plus for these drives is the fact that they can also read CDs (both software CDs and writable CDs). This makes them the most versatile type of optical drive presently available.

The upgrader thinking of buying a DVD drive will find that they are available in three versions: read-only, writable, and rewritable. The decision of which one to go for is based on the same reasons for choosing between the various versions of CD drives.

The issue of DVD formats also needs to be considered. Currently, there are three of these.

DVD- – introduced in 1999, this format is supported by Panasonic, Toshiba, Apple, Hitachi, NEC, Pioneer, Samsung and Sharp. It is available in write-once versions (DVD-R) and rewrite versions (DVD-RW).

DVD+ – this is a more recent format that was introduced in 2002, and is supported by Philips, Sony, Hewlett-Packard, Dell, Ricoh, Yamaha and others. As with DVD-, write-once (DVD+R) and rewrite (DVD+RW) versions are available.

Hot tip

Another advantage of DVD writers is that they write data faster than CD writers do. See page 99 for more on this.

97

Hot tip

There are drives on the market (combination drives) that are capable of using all three formats.

DVD-RAM – a DVD-RAM disc is very similar to a hard drive in that files can be dragged & dropped. This format also offers faster data access and higher levels of reliability than the + and - formats.

However, DVD-RAM discs can be read only in a DVD-RAM drive – the format is not compatible with DVD+ and DVD- drives.

Hot tip

If your primary purpose for buying a DVD drive is long-term data storage, consider one of the DVD-RAM drives. DVD-RAM discs have the highest life expectancy of all the formats. Furthermore, the drives themselves provide data protection facilities, e.g. the marking of bad sectors. These features make DVD-RAM the most reliable format.

Hot tip

The DVD+ format is more advanced than DVD-. It offers faster write speeds, slightly higher disc capacity, and in-built data correction. However, DVD+ discs are more expensive than DVD- and the format is generally considered to be less compatible with home and car DVD players.

Summary

So which one do you go for? For general purpose use, the choice is between DVD+ and DVD-. While there are technical differences (see margin note) between them, to all intents and purposes, they can be considered to be the same. So either will be fine. In any case, most current DVD writers are compatible with both formats.

Users who write, and access, written data frequently will be best served by the hard drive-like qualities of the DVD-RAM format. This format is also the best one for long-term data storage purposes due to its reliability. Remember that it does have compatibility issues with other formats, though.

Blu-Ray/HD-DVD Drives

These devices have been available for about a year now but at prohibitive prices. However, once these fall to an acceptable level, DVD will be consigned to history.

Both formats offer huge storage capacities: Blu-Ray discs can hold 25 GB (50 GB with dual-layer) of data, and HD-DVD 15 GB (30 GB with dual-layer). Future generation discs are expected to hold up to 200 GB.

Why the need for all this capacity? The arrival of High-Definition TV (HD-TV) is the answer. Discs offering this level of capacity will be able to hold two hours of high-definition video; enough for a full-length movie.

As far as PC users are concerned, apart from being to watch movies, either format takes data storage options to a completely different level. For example, you will probably be able to back up your entire system on a single disc.

Early indications indicate that Blu-Ray will win the battle between the two rivals, the main reason being the considerably higher disc capacity that it offers.

Buying a CD/DVD Drive

Having decided what type of drive you want, the next thing is to take a look at these devices and see what they actually offer. The following are the factors you need to consider:

Interface

The vast majority of drives currently on the market use the ATA interface (with an extension known as ATAPI). They are also available with USB, FireWire, SCSI and SATA interfaces (the latter two offering *potentially* faster data transfer rates - see margin note).

Read/Write Speeds

The speed at which a drive reads and writes is indicated by "x" ratings in the specifications. Usually, these are also marked prominently on the packaging, as shown below.

Using this as a typical example, the first figure, 40x, is the speed at which the drive writes to a CD-R. The second, 12x, is the speed at which it writes to a CD-RW, and the third figure, 48x, is its read speed.

However, for these figures to have any meaning, you need to know what the x represents. In the case of CD drives, it represents 150 KB/s. So the CD drive in our example above has a CD-R write speed of 6.0 MB/s (150 x 40).

DVD drives also use this convention. You will notice though, that the x ratings are much lower, typically, 16x, 4x, 16x. On the face of it, this would seem to indicate that DVD drives are slower than CD drives. However, they are actually much faster, and this is because the x represents 1.32 MB/s (as opposed to 150 KB/s with CD drives). So a 16x rating indicates a write speed of 21 MB/s.

Hot tip

The interface used by the drive is something that you don't need to worry about unless you are looking to "future-proof" your system. The ATA interface, which is used by most drives is quite capable of running the drives currently on the market at their full potential.

99

Don't forget

The lower x ratings of DVD drives do not mean that these drives are slower than CD drives. They read data just as quickly and actually write data more quickly.

...cont'd

Specifications

Specs to look out for include:

Writing Mode – a very important factor in the performance of an optical drive is the maintenance of a constant data transfer rate across the entire disc. To achieve this, manufacturers use one of three methods: Constant Linear Velocity (VLC), Zoned Constant Linear Velocity (ZCLV) and Constant Angular Velocity (CAV). All you need to know here is that budget and mid-range drives use the CLV or ZCLV method, while top-end models use CAV.

Access Time – this is the time needed to locate a specific item of data on the disc. This metric is measured in milliseconds and you should look for a figure no higher than 100 ms.

Buffer Size – optical drives use a buffer to ensure that data flows to the disc smoothly and without interruption during the writing process; this helps to eliminate errors. Typically, drives are supplied with a 2 MB buffer and this is the minimum that you should accept. High-quality drives have buffers as large as 8 MB.

Recommended Media

The build quality of CDs and DVDs varies widely and some drives have trouble with low-quality discs. To enable users to avoid this potential problem, most manufacturers provide a list of media recommended for use with their drives, as shown below:

Recommended Media		(All DVD-RW and CD-RW media is rewritable up to 1,000 times)
DVD+R	16X	Taiyo Yuden, Verbatim/Mitsubishi
	8X, 4X	Maxell, Ricoh, Taiyo Yuden, Verbatim/Mitsubishi
DVD+RW	4X	Ricoh, Verbatim/Mitsubishi
DVD+R DL	8X, 4X	Verbatim/Mitsubishi
DVD-R	16X, 8X, 4X	Maxell, Taiyo Yuden, TDK, Verbatim/Mitsubishi
DVD-RW	4X, 2X	TDK, Verbatim/Mitsubishi
DVD-R DL	4X	Verbatim/Mitsubishi, Victor
CD-R	48X	Maxell, Taiyo Yuden, TDK
	40X	Ricoh
CD-RW	32X, 24X	Verbatim/Mitsubishi
	10X, 4X	Ricoh, Verbatim/Mitsubishi Chemical

Dual-Layer Technology

This DVD technique doubles the maximum storage capacity of a DVD to 8.5 GB. However, dual-layer discs can only be written and read by a dual-layer drive. Also, 8.5 GB dual-layer discs currently cost three times as much as a single-layer 4.7 GB disc, which makes them poor value for money.

Installing a CD/DVD Drive

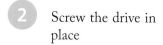

1 Slide the drive into the drive bay from the front (if you try doing it from the back, the PSU will block access)

Hot tip

With some drives an audio cable is not necessary as they use the interface cable to make the connection to the sound system. These drives use a technology called Digital Audio Extraction (DAE).

2 Screw the drive in place

3 If your drive has an audio cable to connect it to the sound system, plug one end in the socket at the far left

Beware

80-pin interface cables are keyed to make sure they fit correctly. However, the older 40-pin cables are not, so it is possible to fit these the wrong way. If this is what you are using, keep the striped edge on the right.

4 Keeping the striped edge on the right-hand side, plug the interface cable into the drive

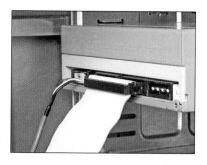

...cont'd

Hot tip

You may need to consult the motherboard or sound card documentation to see where to connect the audio cable.

5 Hook up the power supply

6 Connect the drive to the black socket on the motherboard

7 Connect the audio cable to the sound system

Don't forget

In the case of a second drive, you must set it as the slave. The jumper settings are stamped on the casing.

If you are installing a second drive, perhaps a DVD drive, the first step is to set it as the slave, as shown below. Then as step 4 (on the previous page), plug the slave connector (as shown on page 80, step 3) into the drive. Otherwise, the procedure is exactly the same.

Then boot the PC and your new drive will now be operational.

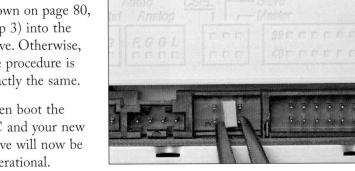
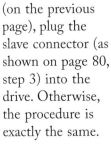

Other Types of Drive

The upgrader looking to add extra storage options to the system has two options, apart from optical drive writers.

Rev Drives

The first is the Rev drive from Iomega. This is basically a souped-up version of the floppy disk drive and works in much the same way. The differences lie in the speed at which it operates, the level of storage capacity offered, and the range of features and options provided.

Hot tip

Rev drives are the perfect solution for people who need a quick and flexible means of storing large amounts of data.

The Rev drive offers some notable advantages over the CD/DVD method of data storage and transfer.

- Unlike writable disk drives, it does not need an associated software program

- It works just like a hard drive does. This means you can save to it from a program's Save As file menu command and by drag and drop. Also, data can be rearranged on the disks

- Data transfer speeds are much higher

- The disks are housed in a tough plastic case, which makes them less susceptible to physical damage

- It provides a range of features, such as password protection and integrated backup facilities

- Much higher storage capacity

Hot tip

A very useful feature offered by Rev drives is password protection.

...cont'd

The Rev drive is designed for users who have large-scale backup requirements. In operation, it has data transfer speeds approaching that of a hard drive, and disks are available in capacities of 35 GB, 70 GB and 120 GB. These factors make it one of the best backup solutions currently on the market.

Beware

Media for Rev drives are extremely expensive on a dollar/capacity ratio compared to other types of storage media.

The only drawback is the cost: the drive and disks are extremely expensive, although the disks are available in packs, which does bring the cost down.

Tape Drives

Tape drives intended for use in a PC are very similar in appearance to a CD or DVD drive. The media they use, as you might expect, is tape and comes in the form of a cassette, much like the old music cassettes that were around years ago.

Typically, these devices are used in corporate environments where massive data backups are carried out on a regular basis. However, users who run a business from home might consider one of these drives (assuming they are prepared to spend the minimum of $600 that they cost).

The tape cassette or cartridge, typically, can hold 20 GB of data, although compression techniques can up this to about 40 GB. The drives have a data transfer rate of around 5 MB/s, which means that a 20 GB cartridge will be filled to capacity in about an hour.

The big advantage of tape drives (once you've recovered from the shock of parting with $600, or more, for one) is that the cartridges themselves are cheap ($10 for a 20 GB tape), and can be reused any number of times.

7

See and Hear More With Your PC

Computer Video Systems

Video systems for computers come in two types: integrated video (built-in to the motherboard), and video cards. Both have pros and cons that make them suitable for some purposes and unsuitable for others. It is essential to know what these are in order to get the one most appropriate for your requirements.

Integrated Video Systems

Integrated video is a feature found on the majority of mainstream motherboards (although it is not always used). It is usually incorporated into the chipset and provides a low-cost video option for both users and manufacturers.

Traditionally, however, the quality of video produced by these systems has not been good. On older PCs, it may not even provide 3D, which is essential for many PC games and certain other types of application. However, modern systems do provide a quality of video that is good enough for all but the most demanding applications.

Another problem is the demands made by integrated video on the computer's resources. Video processing needs a powerful processor and a good supply of memory, and integrated video doesn't have either. Thus, the computer's CPU and memory have to be used, with the result that other parts of the system may be short-changed in terms of CPU and memory resources. Overall, system performance is adversely affected.

Reasons to Upgrade

There aren't any. If your PC is no more than four to five years old, your existing integrated system should be capable of handling whatever you throw at it with the possible exception of 3D games, and heavy-duty applications.

Older computers may well benefit. But as the upgrade is going to involve a motherboard replacement, which turns the job into a major upgrade, a much simpler option would be to just add a video card. Even a low-end model that will cost less than a new motherboard will provide you with all the video processing capabilities required.

Hot tip

For routine, everyday tasks, such as word processing and email, integrated video systems are more than adequate. Recent systems will even play 3D games to a fairly high standard.

Hot tip

The issue of system degradation needs to be put into context. It is a fact that for most people, the performance hit made by integrated systems is negligible and, in fact, will probably not even be noticed. On the other hand, users of poorly specified computers trying to run today's video intensive applications almost certainly will notice.

Video Cards

Video cards provide a much higher level of video quality as they are designed specifically for this purpose. To this end they come equipped with their own processor and memory, which means that the system's CPU and memory are free to carry out other unrelated functions. This results in faster overall system performance.

A bonus is the fact that many video cards have integrated functions, which can help to justify the often high cost of these devices. A hardware DVD decoder is a typical example: this will play DVD movies much better than a software decoder. Bundled software, usually a couple of recent PC games, is often also included in the package.

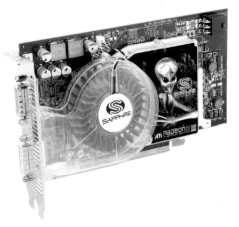

Beware

The big disadvantage of video cards is the cost. Top-end models that provide the latest technology are almost prohibitive in price. Even mid-range models will make a serious dent in your wallet.

There are also issues regarding the heat these devices produce, the noise they make, and the amount of space they occupy.

By providing extra input/output sockets, video cards increase the range of video-related tasks that can be carried out on the PC. Importing video from external devices such as a VHS recorder is one example of this.

Reasons to Upgrade

There are four reasons to upgrade a video card, or add a video card:

1) The existing card has failed

2) You start using an application that demands a high level of video-processing

3) To keep abreast of current video technology, such as the PCI Express interface

4) You need input/output sockets not provided by your existing video system

The Video Card Market

Browse through the video card section of a computer parts retailer or website and you will see models from a large number of manufacturers. What most people don't realize is that many of these cards are almost identical in terms of performance. This is because all of these manufacturers use chips from one of two companies – AMD ATI (the Radeon) and Nvidia (the GeForce),

both of which are very similar (it's the same as CPUs from Intel and AMD).

Because the chip basically defines the quality of the card, it follows that cards from different manufacturers that use the same chip will have

similar levels of performance. So while it may seem that you have a large choice, many of the cards on offer are actually much the

same. Where they do differ is the quality of the control circuitry and the specifications of associated components.

For example, you can buy a card built around the AMD ATI Radeon 9800 featuring 256 MB of memory from one manufacturer, while

another is offering a card with the same chip but with only 128 MB of memory.

Regardless of these differences, however, the quality of the cards output is going to be broadly similar because everything is driven, and controlled by, the chip.

So when differentiating between cards that use the same chip, you need to look at the "extras" provided by each card. These include integrated functions, the number and type of input/output sockets, dual-screen support, the amount and type of memory, etc. Don't forget the bundled software either.

Video Card Specifications

There are so many video card specifications that it would be a herculean task to investigate them all. The following are the main ones and will give you a very good idea of a card's capabilities.

Graphic Processing Unit (GPU)

The GPU is the core of the video card – it determines what it can do and how well it will perform. There are dozens of specifications relating to this device but the main one is its clock speed.

Top-end cards will run at 650 Mhz, mid-range cards at 500 MHz, and low-end cards at 300 MHz.

Memory

Memory is used to store graphics data temporarily and the faster and larger it is, the better the performance of the video card. There are several considerations here as shown in the table below:

Memory	Low-End	Mid-Range	Top-End
Capacity	64 to 128 MB	256 to 512 MB	768 MB to 1 GB
Type	DDR	GDDR 2 and 3	GDDR 4
Clock Speed	500 MHz	1 GHz	2 GHz
Interface	128-bit	256-bit	512-bit
Bandwidth	28 GB/s	57 GB/s	128 GB/s

RAMDAC

The Random Access Memory Digital-to-Analog Converter is a chip that converts the digital signal received from the graphics processing unit (GPU) to an analog signal that is compatible with the monitor. The faster it does this, the better the card's performance. Look for a figure of at least 300 MHz. Good video cards will have a RAMDAC rated at 400 MHz.

Texture Fill Rate

The fill rate indicates the speed at which the card can render a scene. It is a very useful indicator of a video card's capabilities and top-end cards will have a fill rate of around 80 billion pixels per second. Low-end cards will come in at around one billion pixels per second.

Hot tip

A good indicator of a video card's capabilities is the type of memory it uses. Top-end cards use DDR3 and DDR4.

Hot tip

When looking at video card specs, you will notice that some of them have two Ramdacs. These cards provide support for two monitors.

Other Factors to Consider

Input/Output Ports

Quite apart from the quality of video they produce, video cards also increase the user's options by allowing external video devices to be connected to the PC via its ports.

S-Video Port   VGA Port   DVI Port

The VGA (used to connect the monitor) and S-Video (used to connect external devices) ports are standard with virtually all cards.

There are many cards around though, that do not provide a DVI (Digital Video Interface) output. Users of LCD monitors (which are digital devices), or those planning to buy one, should get a card with one of these as they provide a high quality digital signal.

Note that while it is possible to run an LCD monitor from the VGA port, the analog VGA signal has to be converted to a digital one, and the conversion process can result in a slight reduction in picture quality.

Some of the latest top-end cards also offer a High Definition Multimedia Interface (HDMI) socket. This is a new interface standard for consumer electronics devices that combines HDCP-protected digital video and audio into a single connector.

DirectX

DirectX is a program interface designed to allow programmers to write applications without knowing exactly what hardware will be used to run them. Without going into the details, it provides a way of making an application compatible with as many different types of computer setup as possible.

Most multimedia applications (3D games in particular), and applications containing an element of multimedia, are written around a specific version of DirectX and require it to be installed on the PC to function properly.

Interface

Most video cards currently use the AGP (Advanced Graphics Port) socket on the motherboard to connect to the system. This is a high-speed data bus designed specifically to handle the huge amounts of data associated with video.

However, AGP is now being phased out in favor of the newer PCI Express interface, which has a data transfer rate twice that of AGP (PCI Express 2 is four times as fast). Most video cards now coming on to the market use this new interface.

The potential problem for upgraders, is that PCI Express requires a PCI Express compatible motherboard (not to mention the bother of installing it). So unless you really do need the ultimate in video performance, it may be as well to wait until you can justify a motherboard upgrade. Then will be the time to go for PCI Express.

Power Requirements

This will be an issue only if you are considering one of the top-end cards. These devices use a lot of power and it may be that your PC's power supply unit (PSU) is simply not up to the job. If it isn't, it may blow and probably take your CPU and memory with it.

Some of these cards require a 450 watt (or higher) PSU and it is a fact that most PCs are fitted with 300-400 watt PSUs. All the manufacturers advise what power rating their cards require in the specifications. Be sure to check this out because you may need to upgrade this device as well.

Heat

High-end video cards generate a lot of heat and PCs do not like it. Excess amounts can result in components failing long before they should and it is also a major cause of system instability. While the cards themselves are adequately cooled by fans and heatsinks, the heat is merely shifted to other parts of the system case and can cause other components to overheat.

Therefore, along with your new card, you may also need to install an extra fan or two (most cases have mounting points for these).

Hot tip

Those of you who are looking to upgrade an AGP video card, or to add one, should be aware that this interface comes in various speeds – 1x, 2x, 4x, and 8x (currently, the fastest).

The AGP speed offered by the card must be supported by the motherboard. If it is higher, the card will still work but only at the maximum speed supported by the motherboard.

Beware

Another factor that may need to be considered when buying a top-end video card is its physical dimensions. These cards come with massive cooling systems that can block access to the nearest PCI socket. If all yours are in use, you may have to remove one of the devices from your system to make room for the video card. This is something that should be checked out in the card's specifications.

Installing a Video Card

Beware

Before you install a new video card, you are well advised to uninstall the driver for the old one, particularly if you are switching from AMD ATI to Nvidia, or vice versa. This will prevent possible initial configuration problems.

1 Locate the colored AGP or PCI Express slot. This is above the white PCI slots

Hot tip

High-end video cards are heavy and bulky devices due to the massive cooling systems that they use. To prevent them slipping out of the slot, many motherboards these days supply a retaining clip.

2 Open the retaining clip (see margin note)

3 Fit the board into the socket. When it is fully inserted, the retaining clip will close automatically

Don't forget

When you've fitted the new card, its driver will need installing from the installation disk. Then go to Display in the Control Panel and set up the card according to your requirements.

4 Screw the backplate to the chassis

Video Capture Devices

Video, in all its various forms (viewing, recording, editing, etc) is currently one of the most popular applications with PC users. One of the first questions people new to this ask is "How do I get the video into my PC?".

The answer is with the aid of a video capture card. There are several types of this device and each have their pros and cons. The following will help you to decide which one is best for your purposes.

TV Tuners

As the name might suggest, these devices are concerned primarily with allowing you to watch television on your PC, either full-screen or in a resizable window.

Available as either PCI cards or external models, they can display video from a variety of sources. These include standard TV antennas, cable networks, DVD players, camcorders and video recorders.

However, these devices can also be used to record TV (using the PC's hard drive as the recording medium), and to capture video from other types of video device.

TV tuners do have their limitations, however. Very few of them provide a TV-out facility, which other types of capture card do. Also, recording formats offered can be limited; often only MPEG-2, which does not provide high-quality video.

That said, if your requirements in terms of video quality and features are not particularly high, these devices are adequate. For watching TV, they are fine. If you intend to do a lot of video work though, or require high-quality output, a specialized video capture card will be a better option.

Hot tip

Anyone buying a TV tuner with the intention of watching a lot of TV on the PC should choose a model that includes a remote control. Otherwise, you will have to get up and use the mouse or keyboard every time you want to switch channels or adjust the volume.

Beware

Low-end TV tuners are well known for locking-up PCs. If you do not want to be constantly rebooting your computer, resist the temptation to save a few dollars.

...cont'd

Beware

Associated sound can be an issue when using a video card to import video. Many of them do not have native support for sound and rely on the PC's sound system to do the job. With this type of setup, getting the sound to synchronize with the video can be problematic.

Hot tip

1394 sockets provide a high-speed FireWire connection for digital camcorders. This is a very useful option (if you use a camcorder) that is lacking in most home computer systems.

Video Cards

Most video cards provide video capturing facilities. Some also come with an integrated TV tuner. As with TV tuners though, video cards are designed with one specific purpose in mind; anything else they offer is of lesser importance, and thus may also be of lesser quality.

Another problem is that with the current need to provide both VGA and DVI outputs, video cards simply do not have enough room on the back plate to accommodate the full range of sockets necessary to connect all the various types of video device. In most cases a video in/video out (S-Video) socket is all you will get.

Video Capture Cards

For those who are serious about working with video, a dedicated capture card is by far the best option. These devices are also available as external models (shown below) that connect to the system via a USB or FireWire port.

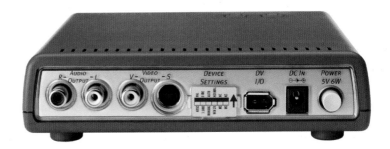

Apart from the higher level of overall quality provided, you will also get much more in the way of connectivity options, such as Mic, Line out, Composite Video Input, S-Video Input, and 4- and 6-pin 1394 (FireWire) sockets.

Other advantages include:

- A higher range of input and output formats

- Faster data transfer rates

- Higher capture resolutions and color depth capabilities

- The ability to export video as well as import it

PC Entertainment Centers

If your reason for upgrading is general entertainment rather than something specific, such as gaming or running graphics applications, you can really push the boat out and go for a PC entertainment center.

These come in two types: a) a purpose built unit, and b) a collection of home entertainment devices connected to, and controlled by, a PC. Both provide the following:

- TV
- DVD video
- CD audio
- Digital video recording (using the hard drive as the medium)
- Standard PC functions

The advantage of a purpose built unit is that with the exception of the speakers and the TV, everything (the PC, DVD and CD players) is housed in one compact unit. Not only is this a real space-saver; aesthetically, it looks much better – PCs are not the most attractive things to have in your living room.

They do have several drawbacks, though. Firstly, buying one of these is more than a simple upgrade – they are not cheap. Secondly, being, essentially, a PC that requires cooling and hence a fan, they make more noise than might be acceptable in a communal room. Thirdly, for close-up PC operations, such as word-processing, the Internet, etc, the low resolution of a standard CRT TV will be inadequate. This means also buying a high-definition LCD monitor or TV (a wide-screen model, assuming you watch DVD movies – and who doesn't these days?).

Building one yourself is a much cheaper option as you already have the PC and probably the other devices as well. All you need is a video capture device with the necessary inputs/outputs and you're in business.

The disadvantage is that the PC will usually have to be moved into the living room so that your TV, music system and CD/DVD players can be connected to it.

Hot tip

Purpose built entertainment centers are expensive. However, they do combine the various devices into one unit, all of which can be controlled with one remote control.

Hot tip

If you are prepared to run extra cabling, your entertainment devices can be connected to a PC in a different room.
   A better option is to build a wireless home network. In conjunction with a portable PC, such as a laptop, you will be able to control the system from any location in the house.

Computer Sound Systems

Integrated Sound

Virtually all motherboards provide an in-built sound system and the ones supplied with motherboards built in the last four or five years or so are actually very good, offering features such as support for multiple-speaker setups, DirectX, EAX and DirectSound 3D.

However, they do have three inherent disadvantages.

1)   They are prone to picking up electrical interference from other motherboard components. This results in a low signal-to-noise ratio, which manifests itself as pops, clicks and buzzes in the output signal

2)   Due to space restrictions on the motherboard's input/output panel, they do not provide the full range of sockets

3)   Integrated systems do make a hit on overall system performance as they rely on the CPU to do all the number-crunching. While the effects are negligible, they are, nevertheless, there

Accordingly, integrated systems are not suitable for the following applications:

●   High-quality sound reproduction

●   Music mastering

●   Hardcore gaming

Users with an interest in any of these will need to install a separate sound card. A possible exception is gaming, depending on the degree of sophistication required (see margin note).

However, for all other purposes, an integrated sound system will be perfectly adequate.

With regard upgrading an old integrated system to a more recent one that offers better quality and more features, this really doesn't make any sense as it will mean replacing the motherboard. A much easier (and cheaper) option, would be to simply install a sound card. A mid-range, or maybe even a budget model, should do nicely.

Beware

As with video, integrated sound systems do have a slightly adverse effect on system performance. Those of you upgrading with the intention of increasing the speed of the PC should be aware of this.

Beware

The main sound requirement for gamers is 3D surround-sound, which requires 3D and speaker connection support. While current integrated systems provide both of these, the quality of 3D sound they offer is not as realistic as that offered by dedicated sound cards. The bottom line here is that if you want the best quality surround-sound, you will need a sound card. Otherwise, a recent integrated system will be adequate.

Sound Cards

Sound cards are available with a range of specialized features and options, and if you're not careful, you could end up buying one that is not ideal for the task in hand.

Games and DVD Movies

For those of you who are seeking to enhance your game-playing or DVD movie experience in terms of sound, the quality of a sound card's output is of less importance than its ability to create the illusion that you are in the middle of the action literally. For example, if a game character walks behind you, his footsteps should sound as though they are coming from over your shoulder.

To be able to do this, the sound card must provide the following:

- Multiple-speaker support – each pair of speakers requires a line-out socket. So a five- or six-speaker system will require three of these, and a seven- or eight six-speaker system will require four

- 3D sound – also known as Positional Audio, this technology accurately recreates the relative positioning of sound in a three-dimensional environment. The de facto standard is currently Creative's EAX. Also popular is Sensuara's 3DPA

For gamers, DirectX is important and the card should support the version used by the games. Also important is the number of simultaneous sounds the card can process (these are referred to as channels in the specifications). If the application throws more of these at the sound card than it is designed to handle, the system's CPU has to help out, which makes a hit on overall system performance. The game's frame rate may also be adversely affected. 32 channels is a reasonable starting point; anything higher is good.

Beware

Gamers need to be aware that some low-end sound cards actually use the computer's CPU to do the processing. With systems running a low-end CPU, this can result in a lower frame-rate that reduces the "smoothness" of gameplay. Integrated sound systems, no matter how highly specified, tend to cause the same problem.

117

Hot tip

The term "channels" is also used to describe the number of speakers that can be connected to a sound card. For example, a three-channel card can support six speakers: two for each channel.

...cont'd

Music Systems

With the addition of a high-quality sound card and speakers, a

PC can be turned into an audio system every bit as good as a purpose-built unit. Furthermore, it will offer many more options, such as editing, disc writing, and storage facilities.

Although it may be desirable in such a system, 3D sound will be less important than the fidelity (purity) of the sound card's output. This is determined by the following specifications:

- Bit-Depth – this describes how much of the original sound file is reproduced by the card. High bit-depth means high-fidelity and dynamic range. CDs use a bit-depth of 16, so if your music collection is stored on this type of media, you need a 16-bit sound card. DVDs use a bit-depth of 24

- Sampling Rate – this determines the range of frequencies that can be converted to digital format by the sound card, and thus the accuracy of the reproduction. A good card will offer a sampling rate of at least 48 KHz

- Signal-To-Noise Ratio – this is a measure of how "clean" a sound signal is. The higher the amount of background noise (electrical interference, etc), the lower the signal-to-noise ratio. Low-end sound cards will have an SNR of some 75 decibels, while top-end cards will offer 100 decibels

- Total Harmonic Distortion – this is a measurement of the noise produced by the sound card itself during the process of converting the analog signal to a digital signal. A good quality card will have a THD of no more than 0.01%

Hot tip

The most important specifications are bit-depth, which relates to the amount of data reproduced, and the signal-to-noise ratio, which relates to the amount of background noise (hiss).

118

One problem inherent in all computers that can spoil an otherwise high-quality sound signal is electrical interference from other components. There are two ways to minimize this:

1)   Isolate the sound card as far as possible (see page 120)

2)   Buy a sound card that comes with a break-out box as shown below

This unit either fits into a spare drive bay or sits on the desktop. It eliminates electrical interference by converting the analog signal to digital form before it is sent to the card in the PC.

Hot tip

Sound cards that come with a break-out box provide higher signal-to-noise ratio's than those that don't. This is important for those who require as clean a signal as possible.

Music Creation

Sound cards for musicians are the most complex of all. Not only must they provide a high-quality signal, they must also offer music mastering features, such as preamplifiers, synthesizers and wave-mixers.

These cards almost always come with a break-out box as described above. Not only does this eliminate the issue of noise, the box also provides the full range of input/output sockets. These include balanced analog inputs/outputs, digital inputs/outputs in S/PDIF, ADAT, FireWire and MIDI, and a Phono (stereo) input. These cover virtually all types of device.

Hot tip

S/PDIF connections are used for transferring digital data, and are found on most consumer video equipment. A sound card that includes this connection will ensure that users are able to hook-up their PCs to these devices.

Installing a Sound Card

1 Maneuver the card into position

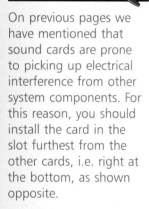

2 Slide the card into the PCI slot and press it home

3 Screw the backplate to the chassis

Speaker Systems

A good set of speakers is an essential part of a high-quality sound system. You may have the best sound card in the galaxy but if it is connected to a cheap speaker system, you will get poor sound.

PC speakers are available either as a pair (as supplied by most PC manufacturers) or as a multiple-speaker system. The type of setup you go for depends on the intended use.

Music buffs who simply want high-fidelity will be best served by a pair of high-quality stereo speakers – a surround-sound system is not necessary.

Gamers and DVD movie fans who want surround-sound will need a multiple-speaker system, as shown below. When buying one of these, don't forget to check that your sound system is capable of fully utilizing it. There's no point in buying a 7:1 speaker system if you have only three line-out jacks.

Whichever type of setup you go for, considering the following specifications will ensure that your chosen speakers are up to scratch.

Hot tip

Surround-Sound speaker systems range from 2:1 (one large subwoofer for bass reproduction, and two smaller satellites – one for mid-range and one for treble reproduction) up to 8:1 (one sub-woofer and seven satellites).

- Frequency Response – this is the range of frequencies that the speakers can reproduce. The closer it is to the 20 Hz (bass) and 20 KHz (treble) thresholds, the better the output quality

- Sensitivity – this is sometimes referred to as Sound Pressure Level and indicates the efficiency with which the speakers convert power to sound. Look for a figure of at least 90 decibels

- Wattage – while this is not an indication of quality, it is a fact that speakers with a high wattage rating do generally produce better sound

Hot tip

Speaker wattage is rated in two ways: peak power and continuous power. The manufacturers like to emphasize the former as this is the higher of the two figures. However, buyers should be more concerned with the continuous (RMS) power rating as this gives a more accurate indication of the speaker's capabilities.

Speaker Installation

Installing PC speakers is simply a matter of plugging them into the sound system's output jacks. To make sure you get this right, most current sound cards and speakers use color-coded connections.

Front speakers plug into the green, rear speakers into the black, and center and side speakers into the orange sockets.

Positioning Speakers

To get the best effect out of surround-sound systems, the speakers must be optimally placed. While there is a large degree of personal preference involved here, the following illustration of a 7:1 speaker system setup is a good guideline.

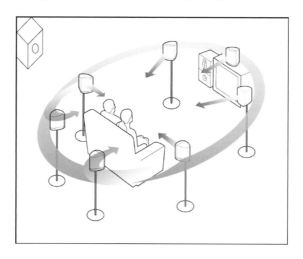

Firstly, the sub-woofer: this is not critical as bass is non-directional. However, the best results will be obtained from placing it next to a wall or in a corner.

The center speaker should be placed on top of the monitor or TV, and the front-right and front-left speakers to either side and angled towards the listener.

Two speakers should be placed on either side and the final two at the rear.

Hot tip

If your sound card or speaker connections are not color-coded for easy identification, refer to the documentation.

Hot tip

Correct speaker positioning is particularly important in 3D games. In a violent fast-paced 3D world, when a sound is supposed to come from your right-rear flank but seems to come from directly behind you, it could cost you a virtual life.

8 Create a Reliable PC

This chapter focuses on the causes of an unreliable system and the upgrades that can be made in order to resolve these issues.

What Makes a PC Unreliable?

An unreliable PC is one that behaves erratically, does things that it shouldn't do and doesn't do things that it should. Typical symptoms are frequent crashing, locking-up and sudden system reboots, all of which are common causes of data loss. Actions of this type can also result in other problems, such as corruption of the operating system.

Unreliability is caused by either a low-quality, faulty or over-extended item of hardware, or problems with the operating system or a software program. Hardware is the most likely culprit, so we'll look at this first.

The PC's Power Supply

A computer has two different power supplies: the AC input from the wall socket and the DC output from the power supply unit. Both can be the source of problems that make a PC unreliable.

Power Supply Unit (PSU)

These devices are prone to two types of problem and in each case, the cause is bad design and the use of low-quality components; in other words, they are cheap and nasty. Unfortunately, this happens to describe the majority of PSUs supplied by PC manufacturers as part of their systems.

The first problem is that the current they supply tends to fluctuate. This means that the PC is sometimes not getting enough and at other times it is getting too much. If these variations in current exceed the tolerances to which the PC's components are built, it behaves erratically.

The second problem is that they fail (being highly stressed components, this is inevitable), and when they do, they do it in a big way – a loud bang, accompanied by a puff of smoke.

Hot tip

Even if they're OK to begin with, low-end PSUs are much more likely to develop the type of faults that affect a PC's stability.

Beware

PSUs are a part of a computer system that most people never consider; they are much more interested in the CPU speed, the video card and the amount of memory. PC manufacturers are aware of this and use cheap PSUs to cut the cost of their systems.

The result is a surge of current though the system that can, and does, destroy other components. Typically, these are the CPU and memory, and sometimes the hard drive as well (where all your data is kept).

So those of you who need or want a reliable system must make sure that your current PSU is not one of these low-end affairs, and in most cases this will mean upgrading it.

There are, of course, other reasons to upgrade the PSU and these include:

- To supply the extra power requirements of new devices that the existing PSU is incapable of delivering

- To provide the power connections required by devices using new technology, e.g. the PCI Express interface

- To reduce the noise levels of the PC by taking advantage of "silent" PSUs

Whatever your reason for upgrading the PSU, considering the following factors will ensure you buy the right one.

Power Rating

The power supply unit must be capable of providing the power requirements of every component in the system with a bit to spare. The latter is important for two reasons:

1) The PSU (as with any device) will not last very long if it is run continuously at full load

2) Having some spare power capacity will allow you to add extra devices at a later date without having to also buy a PSU with a higher power rating

The table on the next page shows you the approximate maximum power requirements of all the components in a computer system, and this will allow you to calculate the amount of power required by your system.

Hot tip

How do you know if you have a low-quality PSU? Easy – check its specifications to see if it incorporates protection circuitry (see page 126). If it doesn't, you should replace it.

Hot tip

Another specification to take note of is the PSU's efficiency rating. This is the ratio of the amount of power that goes into the PSU compared to the amount that goes out. Efficiency is expressed as a percentage and a good figure to aim at is 65 % - 85 %.

...cont'd

Component	Power Required
Low- to mid-range video card	60 W
High-end video card	100 W
Expansion cards	10 W
ATA hard drive	30 W
SATA hard drive	20 W
SCSI hard drive	40 W
Optical drives	25 W
Floppy drives	5 W
Cooling fans	2.5 W
Motherboard	35 W
256 MB RAM	15 W
High-end CPUs	100 W
Low-end CPUs	50 W
LEDs	1 W

Hot tip

When you've worked out how much power is required by your system, add another 50 Watts to the figure to provide some spare capacity.

Don't forget

The provision of overload protection circuitry is one of the main differences between low- and high-end PSUs. Its importance cannot be overstated.

Protection Circuitry

A good quality PSU incorporates circuits that monitor variables such as temperature and current, and if any of them exceed designated limits the PSU simply shuts down (rather than blowing, as cheap models do). This will, of course, also shut down the PC but no damage is done to its components. Low-end PSUs do not have this feature.

These circuits also offer some protection against fluctuations in the external AC supply, which can be another source of problems.

Cooling

Cheaper PSUs, as supplied by PC manufacturers, will have one cooling fan, which is adequate for normal operating conditions. Better quality PSUs, however, usually have an extra fan, mounted underneath or to the side, which will kick-in when the PSU is highly loaded. This provides extra cooling when it is really needed and can extend the working life of the PSU considerably.

External Power Supply

For those who are seeking system reliability, the AC supply to the PC is another factor that must be considered. External power supplies are subject to a range of faults: these include power surges, line noise and frequency variation all of which can adversely affect the stability of a computer.

Power surges are one of the most common and have a similar effect on a PC as a low-quality PSU. They also stress components and, over time, have a cumulative effect that can result in them failing well before they should.

While there is nothing that you can do about the quality of the signal, there are three levels of protection that you can employ:

1) Install a good quality PSU that has protection circuitry. This usually offers some protection against AC faults as well

2) Fit a power surge suppressor (shown below). These devices "smooth" out momentary increases in the AC signal, thus ensuring the supply to the PC is at a constant level

Courtesy of Belkin Corporation

3) Fit a Line Conditioner. These are a step up from surge suppressors and not only eliminate power surges, but also eliminate electrical interference that causes line noise

For home-PC use, a top-end PSU and a power surge suppressor will ensure both a "clean" AC input to the PC, and protection against damage to other system components in the event of problems with the PSU.

Hot tip

Those of you who do mission-critical work on your PC might consider an Uninterruptible Power Supply Unit (UPS). These units provide a battery powered backup that takes over when the AC supply has failed. Typically, they will supply several hours of power.

127

Heat

Another factor that the upgrader needs to be aware of is that of heat and the effect that an excess amount of it will have on the PC's components. Firstly, it stresses them beyond their design tolerances and, secondly, it makes them operate in an erratic fashion. The former causes damage and the latter causes unreliability.

Excess heat is likely to be an issue only when power-hungry devices are added to the system; the most typical example being one of the latest video cards. These devices generate serious amounts of heat and while they all come equipped with cooling systems that directs most of it away from the device, inevitably much of it remains in the system case. The same applies to high-end CPUs.

Cramming a lot of devices (power-hungry or not) into the case can have the same effect. For example, you may have two hard drives, two CD/DVD drives, a video card, a TV tuner card, a sound card, a modem, and an SCSI or FireWire card.

In either of these situations, it may be necessary to install another cooling fan. Virtually all system cases have mounting points for these, which are usually located at the rear and the top.

In the case of a high-end video card, you may be better off by fitting a PCI fan (shown below). This device plugs into the PCI slot next to the video card where it is ideally situated to keep it cool.

Overheating can also be caused, or compounded, by dust blocking the out-take vents of both the PSU and the system case. A can of compressed air or a good healthy puff will clear this away. Don't forget to do the circuit boards as well; these will be covered by a layer of dust which, in case you didn't know, is an insulator.

Installing a Power Supply Unit

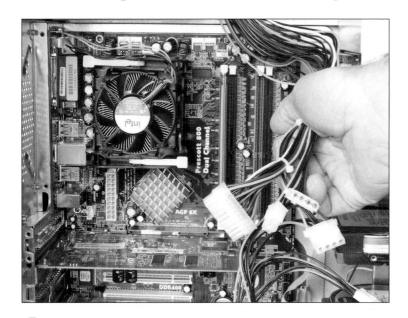

The PSU supplies four different connectors. These are:

Mainboard Power

CD/Hard Drive Power

Floppy Drive Power

ATX 12V

1 Disconnect the existing PSU's cables

2 Unscrew the PSU (at the top rear of the system case)

3 Remove the PSU from the case

4 Install the new PSU by reversing steps 1 to 3

Software

There are two types of software that are well known for rendering a computer system unstable and, hence, unreliable. The first is hardware drivers and the second is malware.

Hardware Drivers

A driver is a small program that acts as an interface between hardware and the operating system. Essentially, it's a set of instructions that tells the operating system how to control and communicate with the associated hardware device. In many cases, it also allows the user to make configuration changes to the device. For example, a printer driver lets you set the print quality, amongst many other things.

One of the problems with drivers is that they often contain bugs (errors), which can cause incompatibility issues with other hardware devices. This can have a knock-on effect that may result in system-wide problems, one of which is general instability.

To resolve this, hardware manufacturers periodically release updated drivers for their products in which the bugs have been fixed. So downloading and installing updated drivers for all your devices as and when they are released will minimize this cause of problems.

Malware

This term is used to describe the multitude of pesky programs that sneak themselves on to a user's PC when certain websites are visited, or are hidden in seemingly legitimate programs. These include spyware, which sends details of the user's PC back to the maker, adware, which opens advertising pop-up windows in the user's browser, and hijackers, which take over the user's browser and redirect all searches to specific sites.

Apart from being extremely irritating, these programs can have a seriously adverse effect on the performance and reliability of the PC. While it is possible to remove them, prevention is much easier than the cure. To stop websites downloading to your PC without your knowledge, you need to install Internet Explorer 7 or Internet Explorer 8 if you're running a version of Windows prior to Vista.

Also, do not install freeware and shareware programs downloaded from the Internet (see margin note).

Beware

Hardware drivers are a particularly important issue for users of Windows XP and Windows Vista. These operating systems are renowned for having compatibility problems with drivers designed for previous versions of Windows. For this reason, you should make sure that all your devices use drivers designed to work with your operating system.

Beware

Those of you who download free and shareware applications should be aware that in many cases the program will have an unwelcome attachment. Software, music and movie files obtained via the file-sharing networks are another source of these programs. It is essential that you scan downloads of this type with both anti-virus and malware removal programs.

9 Improve Your Input Options

Input devices include the mouse, keyboard and game controllers. These devices come in a range of models designed for different applications.

The Mouse

Not so long ago, virtually all mice were very similar in shape and color (a bland beige), and were limited in terms of functionality. This is no longer the case; nowadays these devices are available in a range of colors and ergonomic designs that make them more interesting in a visual sense, not to mention being easier to use.

More importantly, they now use the more efficient optical technology that has replaced the old ball and wheel mechanical system. This works by using an LED (Light Emitting Device) that bounces light off the work surface. The reflected light is processed, and if any changes are detected, the new coordinates are passed to the computer.

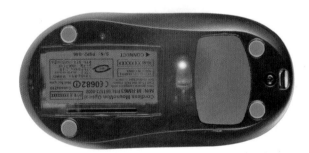

LED sensor on the underside of the mouse

The result is much smoother operation (ball and wheel mice pick up dirt that inhibits movement), and a greater degree of accuracy. Anyone still using the old fashioned type should definitely spend the few dollars that a new optical mouse will cost.

Another option is to go for a cordless mouse. These use radio frequency technology that does away with the need for a cord. Not only does this tidy up the desktop, it also allows the mouse to be used from further away. The drawback is that they are battery powered (see margin note).

Those of you who need even more accuracy have two further options. The first is a laser mouse: these devices are a step up from standard optical mice and replace the LED with a laser beam. The MX™1000 from Logitech (shown below) is an example of this breed of super-mouse.

This device has some 20x more sensitivity to surface detail (tracking power), which makes it ideal for those who need a high level of precision.

Other features include a tilting center wheel for side-to-side scrolling, cruise control for speed-scrolling up and down, and one-click zoom. All-in-all, a superior beast.

The second option is the trackball type of mouse. These are basically an up-ended mouse where the user positions the pointer by rotating the ball with a finger.

Apart from offering a high level of control, they are also ideal for those with hand or wrist disabilities, as they can be operated with a single finger.

A further advantage is that they can be used on any surface as the ball doesn't come into contact with it.

They do, however, take a bit of getting used to.

Hot tip

Laser mice can be used on any type of surface; even glass doesn't faze them.

Don't forget

For applications that require a high degree of precision, laser and trackball mice are the way to go.

133

Keyboards

For general purpose use, keyboards supplied by PC manufacturers get the job done. However, they don't look any thing special, their key action is not the nicest, and they have limited functionality. If you are using one of these to do serious amounts of typing, upgrading to a high-quality model is highly recommended.

One of the things you'll notice is how much more positive and responsive the action of the keys is. This is due to the fact that

good keyboards use a mechanical key system as opposed to the membrane system used by their lesser siblings. Each key is assigned its own switch, which makes an audible click when depressed. When it is released, it springs back into place quickly.

In a membrane keyboard, all the keys sit on a sheet of plastic. This is imprinted with a metallic pattern that, when touched by a key, acts like the switch in a mechanical keyboard and sends the "key depressed" signal to the computer. This is why these keyboards have a spongy feel to them. It is also why they are much cheaper as they have many less parts inside them.

Also available for serious typists are ergonomically designed keyboards. These are constructed in a way that allows users to hold their hands in a more comfortable, slightly angled position, while typing. This type of keyboard can also help prevent, or alleviate, Carpal Tunnel Syndrome. This is an affliction that affects the wrists.

Taking this concept a bit further are split keyboards that have an adjustable hinge in the middle to vary the angle at which the keys are presented to the user's hands.

Hot tip

For a more pleasant typing experience, go for a mechanical keyboard rather than the cheaper membrane type.

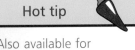
Hot tip

Also available for intensive typists is the Dvorak keyboard. This uses a different key layout that is considered to be more efficient than the QWERTY layout found on standard keyboards.

Comfort is not the only reason to upgrade a keyboard; many of these devices are tailored to meet specific user requirements. For example, those of you who frequently use Microsoft office applications can buy models that have keys relevant to Word, PowerPoint, Excel, etc. Others have keys that control multimedia functions such as play and pause, and Internet and email functions.

Hot tip

If you frequently use the Internet, an Internet keyboard with forward and back buttons, etc, can be handy.

Image reprinted with permission from ViewSonic Corporation

This keyboard from Viewsonic has keys for office, multimedia, Internet, and email applications

Game Controllers

PC games aficionados who need features or levels of precision not offered by the keyboard/mouse combo have four options available to them:

Gaming Keyboards

For some game genres, keyboards are the best type of controller. An example is strategy games, such as Microsoft's Age of Empires, where most of the action is controlled by the keyboard.

Hot tip

For certain types of game, a dedicated gaming keyboard will make life much easier.

While standard keyboards are adequate, much better results will be had from one of the specialized gaming keyboards. These have a multitude of programmable keys that allow the user to customize it to suit specific games.

Most also have an integral joystick, plus illuminated keys that allow games to be played in the dark (hardly essential, but cool nevertheless).

...cont'd

One of the most important features that they offer to gamers is the ability to set up macro commands that combine multiple keystrokes into one. For example, with a standard keyboard, getting a game character to jump forward and kick-out simultaneously will require three keys to be pressed at the same time. A gaming keyboard will do this with one keystroke.

Another type of gaming keyboard consists of a base unit on which can be placed customized keysets designed for use with specific games. If this interests you, visit Ideazon at www.zboard.com.

Joysticks

Joysticks are designed for use with flight simulators, although they can also be used with other genres. An important consideration with these devices is weight and build quality; joysticks are subjected to a lot of abuse and need to be up to the job physically. Another is how securely they fix to the desktop; a joystick that hops around is not going to be of much use.

Another important feature to look for is a twist handle; this gives you rudder control in a flight game.

A good joystick will also have several programmable buttons that allow configurations to be set up for various games using the associated software.

Steering Wheels

Steering wheels are designed specifically for racing games such as Formula One and Nascar. Some even come with a pedal setup for added authenticity.

One of the most important features these devices should provide is force feedback. While this is also available with other types of controller, it is particularly effective in driving games as it lets you "feel" every bump and crash.

The smoothness with which the wheel turns is something else to check – some wheels have a decidedly "clicky" feel to them.

Hot tip

Force feedback technology creates the sense of touch and no decent controller these days would be complete without it.

Also, look for at least six programmable buttons, 240 degrees of wheel rotation and a secure clamping system.

GamePads

These devices are basically a cross between a wheel and a joystick as they provide features common to both but without the high

level of precision. This makes them ideal for use by those who play various types of game.

Any good gamepad will provide at least eight programmable buttons, two analog joysticks (also known as thumbsticks),

and a four-way D pad (used for navigation purposes). Top-end gamepads will have an eight-way D pad for more precise control.

Another consideration is the length of the cord. This should be at least six feet to give you room in which to maneuver.

Hot tip

Game controllers are available in cordless versions that allow the user to sit a lot further back from the monitor. It is a particularly useful feature with gamepads, as a cord flapping about can be restrictive.

Scanners

Scanners are devices that are used to import an image of a picture or document into the user's PC. The difference between low- and high-end models is the speed at which they do it, the quality of the image produced and the level of control offered.

Courtesy of Hewlett Packard

When upgrading this device, or buying one for the first time, you need to consider the following specifications.

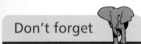

Don't forget

Unless your images are going to be enlarged, the highest scan resolution that you will need is 600 dpi.

Scan Resolution

This is a measure of how much detail is reproduced by the scan process and is expressed in dots per inch (dpi). The higher this figure, the better the quality of the scanned image. The majority of scanners have a maximum dpi of 600 and for most purposes, this is more than enough. The only type of application that requires a much higher scan resolution is image enlarging and for this a high-end model may be needed.

The following table shows what level of resolution is required by the most common applications.

Application	Resolution
Images for commercial printing	300 dpi
Images to be enlarged	1200 dpi upwards
Photos for printing on inkjet printers	300 dpi
Text documents	300 dpi
Line art (drawings, diagrams, etc)	300 dpi
Images for websites	72 dpi

When looking at a scanner's specifications, you may see two figures for resolution – hardware and interpolated. The hardware figure is the one you want; ignore the interpolated figure (see top margin note).

Specifications	
Scanner Type	Flatbed
Image Sensor	CCD
Resolutions, Optical	6,400 dpi (max)
Resolutions, Hardware	6,400 x 9,600 dpi
Resolutions, Interpolated	12,800 x 12,800 dpi
Color Depth	48-bit
Interface	Hi-Speed USB 2.0/1.1

Color Depth

This tells you how many colors the scanner can register and is measured in bits. 24-bits is the minimum required for good color reproduction. However, as virtually all scanners these days can scan at a depth of 48-bits, this isn't really an issue. It's worth checking out though, if you're looking at the low-end of the market.

Optical Density

Also known as Dynamic Range, this indicates how wide a range of tones the scanner can recognize, and is measured on a scale from 0.0 (perfect white) to 4.0 (perfect black).

Most flatbed scanners have an OD around 2.8-3.0 which is fine for photographs. Slides, negatives and transparencies, which have broader tonal ranges, will need a higher OD of about 3.4.

Interface

Most scanners these days use either the USB 2 or SCSI interface, both of which provide much better performance than parallel port or USB 1. Note that SCSI requires an SCSI adaptor to be installed as well, so USB 2 is the recommended option.

Scanning Area

Most flatbed scanners are large enough to scan at letter size. Larger documents will require a scanner with a correspondingly bigger scanning area (and price).

Beware

Interpolated resolution is basically a software enhancement of the true (hardware) resolution, and is achieved by adding extra pixels to the image. While it can improve image quality to a limited degree, it is nowhere near as good as the quoted figure may suggest. Take this with a very large pinch of salt.

Hot tip

Many scanners offer optional accessories that extend their functionality. These include slide and negative attachments, and sheet-feeders.

Hot tip

Scanners that offer one-touch buttons for common tasks can save you a lot of time.

Web Cameras

Traditionally, the only practical uses for these devices has been video links for conferencing purposes, and for recording video "greeting cards" to send to friends and family.

Hot tip

Web cameras are well known for the poor quality video they produce. If you need a clearer image, you may need to buy an Internet camera, as shown below.

However, thanks to the current ease and affordibility of setting up a home wireless network (see page 160), there is now another way to employ them.

In conjunction with a wireless network and a basic software program, a handful of these devices can be used to create a flexible and low-cost home surveillance system. This can be used for a multitude of purposes, such as detecting intruders and keeping an eye on the baby. It can also be easily extended or relocated; for example, moving a camera outdoors to make sure the guys relaying the drive are doing the job properly.

Microphones

Microphones are used as a means of getting the spoken word into a PC. Typical uses are dubbing home movies and voice recognition. They can also be used in conjunction with a PC for voice links over the Internet.

Hot tip

Many Internet telephony companies are now offering low-cost, or even free, Internet calls for people using their software. An example is Skype at www.skype.com.

The latter (known as Internet Telephony) has been around for a while now, but technical issues that have resulted in poor quality connections and unreliability have prevented it from taking off. However, while still far from perfect, the technology behind it has now improved to the extent that it is now a serious option, particularly for overseas calls.

Internet telephony is now being seen as the next major communications revolution and all that's required is a PC, a microphone of reasonable quality and a software program.

10 Data Output Options

In this chapter, we look at the two main devices used to present a computer's data – monitors and printers.

Monitors – CRT v LCD

When buying a monitor, you have two choices: CRT and LCD. But not for much longer; CRTs are slowly but surely being replaced by LCDs.

Even though many gamers and graphics pros still swear by their CRTs, the majority of PC users find LCDs more convenient for a number of reasons. As a result, CRTs have become more and more difficult to find in stores and online, and many major manufacturers have now discontinued their CRT lines altogether.

However, it must be said that CRT monitors still outperform LCDs in terms of color fidelity, viewing angles and resolutions offered. Where LCDs are able to produce a limited number of colors, CRTs are capable of displaying an infinite range. This is very important for graphic artists for example. They also offer unlimited viewing angles. With regard to resolutions, LCDs offer only one (native) that provides a high quality display; other resolutions are produced by interpolation and are not so good. All CRT resolutions are high quality.

On the flip side of the coin, LCDs offer significant advantages over CRTs. They are easier to read in brightly and naturally lit environments; offer sharper text; and are not affected by geometric distortion or flicker (issues with CRTs that can be the cause of eye fatigue and headaches).

Early LCDs were not too good at displaying moving images and ghosting and image blurring were common; a problem that is not an issue with CRTs. However, modern LCDs offer much faster response times, with the result that moving images will be free of ghosting and blurring.

As the vast majority of users are now going for LCDs, this is the monitor we will look at here.

Which LCD Do I Need?

With such a vast range of LCD monitors available, it is important that you consider exactly what you need from your monitor before you part with the cash. The following is a guide:

Home Users

For home users it's a trade-off between price and performance. Extra features such as speakers or USB ports should be taken into account and, depending on the PC's location, aesthetics may be an issue as well.

Important features:

- Price
- Color accuracy
- Clarity, e.g. sharp text
- Aesthetics
- Video connection

Business Users

The important thing for business users is productivity. Extras may be useful but are not essential as are good image quality, and ergonomics for comfortable and extended viewing.

Important Features:

- Large display area
- Ergonomics, e.g. adjustability
- Energy efficiency
- Reliability
- Display quality

Digital Photographers/Graphic Artists

Many monitors are unable to display color accurately and the printer's output will thus be significantly different. This is an important issue for business users working with digital images and so they need high-end LCDs, which offer highly accurate color scales plus color calibration options.

Important Features:

- Color calibration options
- Excellent screen geometry
- Large display area
- High resolution

Hot tip

Some monitors have an anti-reflective screen coating. This helps to reduce glare and ambient light reflection and so provide a brighter, more vivid picture.

Hot tip

LCDs are much easier on the eye. Users who spend long periods at the PC will benefit from this.

...cont'd

Gamers

The primary requirement for gamers is quick response to their key and mouse commands. Image and sound quality is also important but play second fiddle to rapid graphic response.

Important Features:

- Response time
- Color accuracy
- Large display area

Movie Buffs

The requirements for those who watch movies/video on their monitor are similar to those for gamers, plus some.

Important Features:

- Response time
- Color accuracy
- Large display area
- Wide aspect ratio
- Front-panel inputs
- Alternate signal inputs

Monitor Specifications

Specifications to consider are:

Aspect Ratio

The standard aspect ratio for monitors is 4:3, but wide-screen models have one of 16:9 or 16:10. If you intend to watch movies or HDTV in wide-screen format it will be necessary to buy one of these. Note that they are also useful for displaying two windows side by side.

Contrast Ratio

A monitor's contrast ratio is the measurement of the difference in light intensity between the brightest (white) and darkest (black) tones. However, you should be aware that this measurement will vary throughout the screen due to the slight variations in the lighting behind the panel. Manufacturers will use the highest contrast ratio they can find on a screen, so the figure quoted can be somewhat deceptive.

If it is too low, the image will look faded and washed-out, whereas a high contrast ratio will result in a vibrant colorful image.

Resolution

The monitor's native, or fixed, resolution must be suitable for your applications. Note that this will also determine the size of the monitor. 15-inch monitors have a native resolution of 1024 x 768, 17- and 19-inch monitors 1280 x 1024, 20- and 21-inch monitors 1600 x 1200, and 23-inch monitors 1920 x 1200.

So, for example, if you need, or are comfortable, with a resolution of 1280 x 1024, your choice will be restricted to 17- and 19-inch models, assuming you need a high quality display.

Pixel Response Rate

This specification indicates how quickly a pixel can change color and it is measured in milliseconds (ms). The lower the figure, the faster the response rate. A sufficiently fast response rate is critical for eliminating or reducing the blurring effect you might otherwise see in a moving or changing image on an LCD monitor.

In order to eliminate completely any ghosting/blurring, a monitor's pixel response rate must be no higher than 16 ms.

Viewing Angles

CRTs can be viewed from any angle and while the sharper the angle the less you can see, the image itself doesn't deteriorate. This is not the case with LCDs. With these, there is a noticeable loss of image quality when the monitor is viewed from an angle. It is not a major issue but it is, nevertheless, there. Note that the viewing-angle problem is more pronounced as LCD size increases.

Connections

LCDs are digital devices and thus have to convert the PC's analog (VGA) signal before it can be displayed. The conversion process can lead to a slight deterioration in the signal's quality. Most modern LCD monitors provide a digital connection (DVI), which avoids this issue but some don't.

Ideally, the LCD monitor you buy will provide a DVI connection but it isn't critical if it doesn't as analog signal processing is much better than it was a few years ago. Indeed, very few users will be able to notice the difference.

Hot tip

Good quality LCDs have a viewing angle of 160 to 170 degrees. Low-end models have viewing angles as low as 60 degrees.

Hot tip

With some LCDs it is possible to pivot the display, i.e. landscape to portrait. This is an option that can be useful in some types of application, e.g. graphics and CAD.

Other LCDs can be detached from the stand and fixed to a wall. While we can't think of an obvious use for this feature, someone, somewhere, no doubt will.

Installing a Monitor

CRT Monitors

These use the blue VGA connection and connect either to the video card or to the motherboard's integrated video system.

Beware

If your PC has both a video card and integrated video, make sure that you connect the monitor to the right one. This is a very common mistake and is easily done.

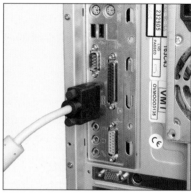

Video card   Integrated video

LCD Monitors

These can use both VGA and DVI connections. If your system has a DVI equipped video card, this is the one to use (shown below). Otherwise, use the VGA connection as shown above.

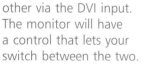

Hot tip

If your LCD monitor has both VGA and DVI inputs, you can use it with two separate PCs. Connect one PC via the VGA input and the other via the DVI input. The monitor will have a control that lets your switch between the two.

DVI output from the video card

Printers

To meet their printing requirements, upgraders have a choice of four types of device. These are:

- Inkjet printers
- Laser printers
- Photo printers
- Multi-function devices (MFDs)

Beware

Manufacturers rate the print speed of their printers in pages per minute (PPM). However, these are taken under optimal printing conditions and do not reflect their real-world performance. Take these with a pinch of salt – the real print speed will be considerably less.

InkJet Printers

Cheap and readily available, these devices are the ideal solution for all-round, or occasional, printing requirements. Print quality, while not the best, is perfectly adequate for most purposes.

They do, however, have some limitations that make them unsuitable for high-quality or large-scale printing.

- Inkjets are not the quickest printers; in fact many of them are painfully slow at anything other than draft quality. For the odd letter now and then they are fine but for more serious printing, the slow print speed can be very restrictive

- Inkjets may be available at low prices but this definitely does not apply to the consumables (ink cartridges, paper, etc). These are highly priced and this is where the manufacturers make their money

Don't forget

If you do serious amounts of printing, an inkjet will be a slow and expensive way of doing it.

...cont'd

- Inkjets can be messy devices and this is due to the fact that they work by literally firing the ink at the paper. It is quite common with these devices for ink to contaminate the platen and rollers, which is then transferred to the paper in the form of smudges and streaks

Should you decide to buy one of these printers, consider the following:

Print Resolution – this is expressed in dots per inch (dpi). Letter quality begins at 300 dpi but a higher figure will be required for the highest quality printing. Photographs print acceptably at 300 dpi. All inkjets provide 300 dpi but the resolution offered will be worth checking if you need really high quality printing.

Print Speed – this is rated in pages per minute (PPM) and as we mentioned on the previous page, it does not give an accurate indication. However, it can be useful as a rough guide when comparing different models.

Paper Handling – mainstream inkjets will print letter size or lower. If you need to print larger documents, you will need to buy a business class inkjet, which will be considerably more expensive. Another thing to look at if you envisage having long print jobs is the capacity of the paper input tray. Low-end inkjets will hold no more than 50 sheets or so; high-end models will hold about 150.

Photo Printers

Due to the popularity of PCs for storing and editing images, photo printers are now extremely popular. These use inkjet

technology but take it to a different level in terms of print quality. One of the ways they achieve this is by using a wider range of colored inks than standard inkjets do. As a result, print quality approaches that of professional print labs.

Photo printers are also much quicker than standard inkjets, which can take an eternity to print a high-quality photo. Another feature they offer is the ability to read directly from flash memory cards, such as those used by digital cameras. This means that the PC is bypassed completely. Many also offer an LCD to view your photos, not to mention editing facilities such as crop, rotate, brightness and contrast adjustment, etc.

Things to look out for when buying a photo printer include:

Ink Cartridges – photo printers use between four and six different inks and generally, the ones that use six will produce higher quality prints than those which use less.

You should also be aware that some use a single cartridge that contains all the inks, so if one color runs out, the cartridge has to be replaced even though the other colors haven't. Therefore, running costs can be cut substantially by choosing a model in which each color is held in a separate cartridge.

Memory Card Reader – if you want to take advantage of the direct printing facility offered by these printers, make sure it can read the type of memory card that you use. In particular, look for PictBridge support (see margin note).

Print Size – many photo printers have a maximum print size of 4 x 6 inches, which is fine for snapshots. If you want larger sizes, say to frame and hang on the wall, you may need a more expensive model.

Laser Printers

Lasers use a completely different technology than inkjets, which produces a higher level of print quality and speed. They also offer much more in the way of features, such as duplexing (the ability to print on both sides of the page) and high-capacity paper input trays. Furthermore, they have much lower running costs.

Traditionally, these devices have been superb at printing text but not so good at color images, as print resolutions were often limited to 600 dpi (which is fine for text). However, with more and more users demanding photo quality from their laser printers, the manufacturers are now providing models that print at 1200 dpi.

Beware

Not all printers with the word "photo" in their name are actually photo printers. Some are merely a general-purpose printer with a few photo printer features, such as direct printing from memory cards or the ability to make borderless prints. Study the specs carefully to weed out the jokers.

Hot tip

PictBridge is a standardized technology that lets you transfer images from the memory card in a digital camera directly to a printer. Print size, layout, date, and other settings can be set within the camera. However, both the printer and the camera must support PictBridge.

...cont'd

Hot tip

One useful advantage provided by color lasers over inkjets, is the ability to print high-quality photos on plain paper – expensive glossy paper is not necessary.

150

Beware

Keep your eyes peeled for laser printers that claim an "effective" resolution of 1200 dpi. This means a real resolution of 600 dpi that has been bumped-up by means of software enhancement. This is a way (much favored by manufacturers of printers (and scanners)), to make their products appear better than they actually are.

While these do produce good-quality color prints, it must be said that low-end color lasers still cannot match an inkjet photo printer.

The price of laser printers has dropped considerably over the last few years and it is now possible to buy a black & white model for around $150, which is less than a high-end inkjet will cost. However, prospective buyers should be aware that if they buy one of these low-cost models, they will be buying at the bottom of the laser market and the performance offered may be no better than that of a good quality inkjet. Probably the only benefit will be lower running costs.

When buying a laser printer, consider the following:

Print Resolution – for text, a dpi of 600 is fine. However, if you intend to print color photos, a dpi of 1200 is recommended. Note that low-end color lasers offer a dpi of only 600.

Consumables – while these are much cheaper than inkjet consumables, you can make further savings by buying a model that has the toner (laser equivalent to inkjet ink) in a separate cartridge. Some lasers have the toner and the drum (which needs to be replaced much less frequently) combined in a single cartridge. As the toner runs out long before it is necessary to replace the drum, being able to replace each individually is more cost-effective.

Memory – lasers come equipped with their own memory. However, low-end models aren't equipped with much, often only enough for small-scale print jobs and low-resolution photo printing. Make sure that the model you buy allows you to install extra memory (not all do), should it be necessary.

Multi-Function Devices (MFDs)

These devices consist of a printer and a scanner, which also combine to act as a copier, and sometimes a fax machine, all incorporated within the same housing.

The advantages offered are convenience (one connection to the PC, one wall socket required), less desktop space than would be required by stand-alone devices, and a cost-saving compared to buying the devices separately.

Along with the lower price, however, you will usually also get lower quality, unless you opt for a high-end model, in which case you will lose the cost-saving. The advice then is to steer clear of MFDs unless: a) space is at a premium, and b) you can afford a high-end model that will meet your requirements. To this end, you should study the specifications for each incorporated device as you would with stand-alone devices.

The bottom line then:

- For high-quality glossy photographs, an inkjet photo printer will be the best choice, unless you are prepared to shell-out $1000 plus for a mid-range color laser. If high-quality text printing is also a requirement, it might be necessary to buy a high-end standard inkjet, or low-end laser printer, as well

- For large-scale text based print jobs, a black & white laser is the recommended option. Even a low-end model will be better than most inkjets, with the added advantage of much lower running costs

- For the busy home office where print jobs are frequent, and use both text and color, a low-end color laser will be a real boon. Not only will printing be quicker and cheaper; more options will be available, such as being able to print on both sides of a page. In short, productivity will be much increased

- If space and/or cost is an issue, and high quality isn't, go for a multi-function device

Beware

A potential problem with multi-function devices is that if they go wrong, the user may lose all the functions that they provide.

Installing a Printer

The usual procedure with modern printers is to install the driver first. Then you connect the device to the computer (demonstrated below) when instructed to do so by the installation procedure. The printer is then configured automatically.

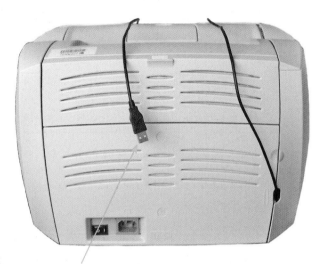

1 Take the USB cable from the printer and connect it to a USB port on the PC

11 Better Network Connections

In this chapter, we investigate Internet connection options. We also take a look at the subject of home networking.

Dial-Up Connections

Those of you still using dial-up modems for your Internet connection have two ways of improving your connection speed. The first is by upgrading to Broadband, which we'll look at on page 156.

The second is to upgrade your existing dial-up modem. Whether this is worth doing or not depends on the age of your PC. If it is five years or more old, you will definitely gain by doing so. If it is less than five years old, you probably won't.

In the former case, your modem will probably be a V.90 model (see top margin note), which means that it is capable of operating at 56 KB/s. This is currently the maximum speed for dial-up modems, so an upgrade will not increase your connection speed. However, it will allow you to take advantage of the benefits offered by the latest modem standard, V.92 (see bottom margin note). If you have a really old PC, the modem could well be a V.34 model, which will have a speed of 33.6 KB/s. In this case, an upgrade will improve your connection speed as well.

PCs less than five years old should already have a V.92 modem (this standard was introduced in 2003). However, it is worth checking that this is actually the case.

The issue of connection speed apart, there are other reasons to upgrade. One is to use your PC as a fax machine, which will require a fax enabled modem (most modems supplied by PC manufacturers aren't). Another is to set up a telephone answering machine on the PC; this will require a voice modem.

Upgrading a PCI card modem to an external modem (shown below) will release the PCI socket for another device.

A further advantage is that external modems have a number of LEDs, which can be useful when troubleshooting connection problems.

Installing a Dial-Up Modem

1 Slide the modem into a PCI socket

Don't forget

To complete the installation, install the modem's driver when back in Windows.

2 Press it home

3 Connect one end of the cable to the modem's output socket

4 Connect the other end to the telephone jack

Broadband Connections

The advantages offered by broadband provide the most compelling reason to throw away the dial-up modem. The following are just some:

Accessibility – with an always-on connection, the Internet becomes literally an extension of the PC. Any site can be accessed with just a couple of mouse clicks.

Reliability – broadband offers a far more reliable connection than dial-up modems do.

Speed – downloads take a fraction of the time needed by dial-up connections. General web navigation is also far quicker.

Telephone – you will be able to make and take telephone calls without having to log off.

Having made the decision to do it, the first step is to sign-up to one of the packages offered by your ISP. Next, you need to acquire a broadband modem. Here, you have two options: a) buy the modem yourself, or b) rent the modem from the ISP. The third step will be the ISP sending a technician round to hook you up to the network. If you are renting the modem, the technician will install it for you while there. Otherwise, you'll have to install it yourself.

You also need to consider the various types of broadband as they all have their pros and cons. The most common is ADSL, as this uses the telephone network. As long as your local exchange is suitably equipped, this will be available. The same applies to ISDN; however this offers much slower speeds.

The best option, if it's available, is cable. This utilizes CATV cable networks (cable TV) and offers speeds of up to around 20 MB/s. It is also the most reliable as most cables are undergound where they are not subject to storm and other types of damage. The next best option is ADSL, which offers speeds similar to cable but is not as reliable. ISDN is the least attractive option as speeds are limited to a maximum of 128 KB/s.

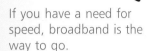

Hot tip

If you have a need for speed, broadband is the way to go.

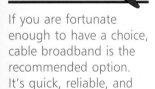

Hot tip

If you are fortunate enough to have a choice, cable broadband is the recommended option. It's quick, reliable, and easy to set up.

Installing a Broadband Modem

The first step is to extend the signal input from its entry point at the house to where the modem is located. For this you will need a suitable length of coaxial cable and the appropriate connectors. If you are tapping into your TV's cable input, you will also need a signal splitter, as shown left. Connect the signal cable to the splitter's input, connect the TV to one output and the modem's cable to the other output. Then run the latter to the modem.

Hot tip

If you are using an Ethernet modem, you will also need an Ethernet adaptor in the PC. There may be one built-in to the motherboard, in which case you will have to install the Ethernet driver from the motherboard's installation disk. Otherwise, you will need to buy and install a separate adaptor.

1 Connect the power cable

2 Connect the interface cable

3 Connect the signal input

4 Connect the modem (a USB modem in this example) to the PC. An Ethernet modem will connect to an Ethernet adaptor PCI card

Beware

When running your new modem for the first time, remember that it may need several minutes to synchronize itself with the network. During this period, you will be unable to access the Internet.

5 Switch the PC on and when back in Windows run the installation disk. In the case of a USB modem, the USB driver required by the modem will be installed automatically. The software will then establish and configure your broadband connection

Home Networking

A network consists of a number of computers that are inter-connected by either a cable (known as a wired network) or a radio link (known as a wireless network). Any type, or combination, of computer can be used in this way. It is also possible to add devices such as printers to extend the versatility of the network.

Hot tip

Users of a networked PC can designate what content on the PC is accessible to other users. This is done via a technique known as file sharing.

A wireless network adaptor

The users of networked PCs have direct access to all the other PCs on the network, thus allowing the contents and resources of each PC to be shared. So if user A needs a file that is on user B's PC, it can be simply copied across – this is extremely convenient. If only one of the PCs has a printer connected to it, all the other PC users can use this printer – this is very cost-effective.

In a home environment, these advantages, and others, can be extremely useful in many ways. One such is the facility to share a single internet connection with a number of PCs located in different rooms. A good example of this in use is the kids using the Internet to do their homework. Son and daughter can both engage in this activity without having to wait for the other to finish. At the same time, Dad can be checking his emails or catching up on the baseball results. The inevitable conflicts that arise from having to share the connection are eliminated.

Hot tip

Wireless hotspots are small localized wireless networks that are connected to the Internet. They are set up in public places, such as airports and hotels. Users with wireless enabled portable PCs can access these hotspots, and then connect to another network anywhere in the world, including their own home network.

If the network is wireless, it is much more flexible. For example, if it's a nice day you can take your laptop out into the garden and work from there. PCs can be moved to different locations without having to reroute cabling. Wireless hotspots (see margin note) enable the user to access the network from literally anywhere in the world.

The advantages and uses provided by a home network are clear. What will be less clear to most people is how to set one up. To find out how it's done, read on.

Building a Home Network

Cable Networks

The traditional method is by using specialized network cable that connects to a network adaptor in each of the networked PCs. With large networks, such as are found in corporate environments, this is no easy task as it requires a thorough knowledge of network topology (types of configuration and associated pros and cons), and devices such as routers and access points.

In a home environment though, it is a relatively straightforward task as each PC is simply linked to the next one. The main problem involves the routing of the cable. If you are handy with an electric drill, and are comfortable with the prospect of pulling up floorboards and recessing the cable into the walls, go ahead. No matter how handy you are though, a certain amount of redecorating will be necessary.

The advantages of this type of network are speed and reliability. Network cable offers the fastest possible data transfer speeds, and once in place the system will be extremely reliable as the cable is durable, and also shielded against electrical interference. The only thing that's likely to go wrong is a dodgy connection to one of the PCs, which is easily and quickly remedied.

Power Cable Networks

A much easier, and less messy, type of system known as HomePlug, uses the house's power cables. This is available in kits consisting of two or more HomePlug adaptors, an installation CD and all the necessary connection cables. All you have to do is plug each adaptor into the nearest wall socket, connect them to network adaptors in the PCs and run the installation CD. As every room has at least one wall socket, there should be no need to install any wiring at all, apart from maybe an extension cable from the socket to the PC.

Beware

Network cable is approximately a quarter of an inch in diameter, so don't think that you will be able to get away with running it under the carpets.

Don't forget

HomePlug networks generally run at approximately 14 MB/s. Compare this with 100 MB/s for cable networks and 54 MB/s for wireless networks. If all you want is to share an Internet connection, and simple file sharing, they are adequate. However, they do not provide enough bandwidth for sharing audio and video files.

Having said that, Devolo (www.devolo. com) offer a high speed HomePlug kit that can run as fast as 85 MB/s.

...cont'd

Beware

HomePNA networks are the slowest of all the various types – 10 MB/s. Accordingly, they are only suitable for very basic networks.

Hot tip

An issue that ought to be considered with regard to wireless networks is that of security. Anyone with suitable radio equipment can easily hack into an unprotected wireless network. While it's unlikely to happen in a home environment, if you do have sensitive data (work documents, for example) on your PC, you should add a layer of protection.

The best method of doing this is to add a hardware firewall to the network, which will block access to it. Another method is data encryption, which can be set up with Windows.

Telephone Wire Networks

A system very similar to HomePlug, called HomePNA, makes use of the telephone wiring in the house. Again, this is supplied in kits comprising a number of adaptors, connection cables and software.

The ease of setting it up depends on whether you have telephone jacks near enough to the PCs to be networked. If you don't though, they are simple enough to install with the aid of extension kits. Plus, the cables can be run under carpets.

Wireless Networks

Also known as Wi-Fi, this is the easiest way to set up a home network, assuming that you are running either Windows XP or Windows Vista. A wireless network can be set up with

other operating systems but it is a more difficult and protracted procedure. The network wizard provided by XP/Vista does the job with a few clicks of the mouse.

All that's required in the way of hardware is a wireless network adaptor for each PC to be networked. This can be either an internal PCI card or an external USB device.

Apart from the ease of setting them up, the great advantages of wireless networks are their flexibility, and the range of uses to which they can be put. With regard to the latter, there are now any number of wireless devices on the market, such as LCD TVs, music systems, and cameras.

By incorporating them into a wireless network, these devices can be simply picked up and moved to wherever they are needed.

12 Fixing Your PC

Initial Steps

In practice, it is virtually impossible to repair a hardware device, particularly circuit boards such as motherboards and video cards. To do so would require specialized electronic equipment, e.g. an oscilloscope, plus the knowledge of how to use them.

Because of this, computer hardware is repaired by the simple expedient of replacement with a working model. This is what repair technicians do and it is dead easy – the difficult part is pin-pointing the faulty component.

One reason for this is the fact that many PC faults can have several causes and this makes it difficult to know where to start. A very useful pointer here is that the majority of faults are actually induced by the user, often as a result of doing something incorrectly, or that shouldn't have been done at all.

So the first thing to do is cast your mind back to what you were doing on the PC prior to the fault materializing. Very often this will provide you with a starting point. The following activities are the cause of most problems.

Installing and Uninstalling Software
Software installation can introduce bugs and incompatibility issues with other software, particularly the operating system. Uninstalling software can also uninstall files needed by other programs.

Using the Internet and Email
The Internet can introduce malware and email can introduce viruses.

Installing Hardware
Hardware drivers are renowned for causing configuration problems with other hardware devices. If the hardware is an internal device, it can also be the cause of heat issues. Another potential cause of problems is dislodging the connections of other components during the installation.

Changing BIOS and System Settings
This can cause a whole range of faults.

Incorrect Shutting Down of the PC
This can corrupt the PC's file system, and Windows startup files.

Hot tip

Faults with hardware devices are actually very rare. In most cases, the problem will be a software issue, such as a corrupted or incorrect driver.

Don't forget

When troubleshooting a PC, it is essential to have a line of attack. Going at it like a bull in a china store will almost always make matters worse.

Troubleshooting Tools

Before you do any upgrading, you should familiarize yourself with the diagnostic and repair tools provided by Windows in case of subsequent problems.

System Restore

Versions of Windows from Me onwards, provide a utility called System Restore. This utility takes "snapshots" (called restore points) of the entire system whenever major changes are made to it, such as a program being installed or uninstalled. These snapshots are saved and can be used to restore the system to the state it was in when the snapshot was taken.

This is an extremely useful way of repairing a fault without having to go to the bother of locating it, and will resolve many software issues. Obviously, it cannot repair a faulty hardware device and if you are certain that this is the case, there is no point in running it. Otherwise, System Restore should be your first move.

Don't forget

System Restore should be used whenever you suspect the fault is software related. Hardware faults, unfortunately, are not so easily resolved.

1. Go to Start, All Programs, Accessories, System Tools and System Restore

2. At the first screen, click "Restore my computer to an earlier time"

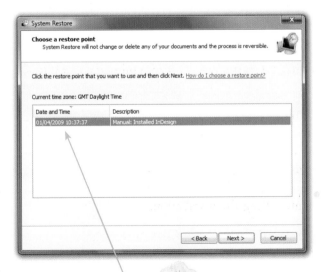

Beware

One caveat with System Restore that you should be aware of is that any programs installed since the restore point was taken will be uninstalled by the restoration procedure. This applies to hardware as well, i.e. the drivers will be uninstalled. Your data, however, will be kept.

3. Select an appropriate restore point and click Next. Windows will restore the system and then reboot to complete the procedure

...cont'd

Device Manager

Technically, this is not a troubleshooting tool. However, it does indicate when a hardware device has a problem and so can be very useful. Access the utility as follows:

1. Windows XP users should go to Start, Control Panel, System. Click the Hardware tab and then click Device Manager. Vista users will find Device Manager in the Control Panel

2. Here you see a list of every hardware device installed on the PC

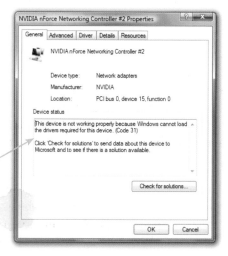

3. Any device with a problem will have a warning symbol next to it

4. Double-click the device to see the nature of the problem and the suggested remedy

Don't forget

If you suspect a hardware fault, the Device Manager is the first place to go. Very often the problem will be a corrupted driver and Device Manager will tell you if this is the case. You will also be able to reinstall the driver from here.

Hot tip

Any device that has a problem is marked with a warning symbol in Device Manager.

Safe Mode

Safe Mode is used to troubleshoot problems that prevent Windows from starting. It works by bypassing the normal Windows configuration, instead loading a "stripped-down" version with a set of basic drivers. This eliminates many potential problems and will usually get Windows running. You are then able to access Windows troubleshooting tools, which will enable you to locate the source of the problem. Access Safe Mode as follows:

1 Boot the PC and immediately start tapping the F8 key. After a few moments, the Windows Advanced Options Menu will open

```
Windows Advanced Options Menu
Please select An Option

Safe Mode
Safe Mode With Networking
Safe Mode With Command Prompt

Enable Boot Logging
Enable VGA Mode
Last Known Good Configuration (Yout Most Recent Settings That Worked)
Directory Services Restore Mode (Windows Domain Controllers Only)

Start Windows Normally
Reboot
Return To OS Choices Menu

Use the up and down arrow keys to move the highlight to your choice
```

2 Using the arrow keys, scroll to Safe Mode and press Enter. Unless there is a serious problem with Windows, it will now start

Chkdsk

Chkdsk is a utility that checks the hard drive for physical errors, such as bad sectors and, more importantly, the PC's file system. It will also repair any problems that it finds. Good indicators of a corrupted file system are general system instability, file copy errors and loss of data. Whenever you experience any of these problems, you should run Chkdsk.

To do it, open My Computer and right-click the C: drive. Select Properties and then click the Tools tab. Under Error checking, click Check Now and then in the new window check "Automatically fix file system errors". Then click Start.

Don't forget

If you are unable to get Windows started, reboot the PC into Safe Mode; this should get it going. However, be aware that when in Safe Mode, Windows will run much more slowly than usual and many of its functions will be disabled. Its troubleshooting tools, such as System Restore and Device Manager, will be accessible, though.

165

Hot tip

Chkdsk should also be run after an incorrect shutdown. This is the most common cause of file system errors.

Make a Windows XP Boot Disk

A PC which refuses to start is one of the most soul-destroying things that can happen to a computer user and most people have no idea of what to do about it. Nine times out of ten, the cause is a corrupted startup file and while there is a way resolving this with Windows, it is far from easy.

A much simpler way is to use a boot disk, which contains copies of critical startup files. To use it, all you have to do is place it in the floppy drive and reboot the PC. Windows will then use the good file on the disk to get itself going. Note that the following applies to Windows XP only.

1 Place a blank floppy disk in the floppy drive and then go to My Computer. Click the hard drive, and on the toolbar click Tools, Folder Options. Then click the View tab

2 Scroll down and check "Show hidden files and folders." A bit further down, uncheck "Hide protected operating system files (recommended)". Click OK. Some grayed-out files will now be visible in the drive window; these are protected system files

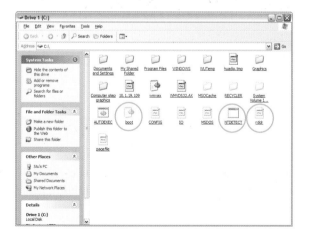

3 Select the boot, NTDETECT and ntldr files. Then right-click, click Send To, and select 3½ Floppy (A:). When the files have been transferred, your boot disk is complete. Label it and put it somewhere safe

The Power Supply

As we have mentioned previously, power supply units are one of the hardware devices most likely to cause trouble. Usually, they leave the user in no doubt – a loud bang accompanied by a wisp of smoke, which is pretty conclusive. However, nothing in life is certain, so if your PC appears to be dead, you have to check the power supply first, bang or no bang.

Before you do, establish that the PC really is dead. There are three things to check:

1) The LEDs at the front of the case are all off

2) The keyboards LEDs are off

3) The power supply unit and CPU fans are not running.

If none of the above are working then the PC is not receiving any power. Troubleshoot by checking the following:

- Confirm that there is power at the wall socket by plugging an appliance such as a hairdryer into it. If the appliance works, the socket is OK

- Bypass any device that is connected between the wall socket and the PSU, such as a surge suppressor or cable extension

- Check the PC's power cable by replacing it with one known to be good (you may have a household appliance that use's the same type)

- Check that the on/off switch at the rear of the PSU hasn't been switched to the off position inadvertently. This is not unlikely if children have been in the vicinity recently

If the computer is still not powering up after carrying out these checks, the power supply unit has failed and will have to be replaced.

Hot tip

PSU faults are not always apparent. As we explained on pages 124-125, these devices can be the cause of fluctuating current to the PC. If you are experiencing an abnormal amount of system crashes or lock-ups, the PSU is one of the first things to check.

Don't forget

Don't overlook the on/off switch on the PSU. What's out of sight is often out of mind. Many users are not even aware that it exists.

System Hardware

By system hardware, we mean hardware devices without which the PC will not start. These are:

- The motherboard
- Memory
- The video system

If any of these are faulty, bootup will stop at the first boot screen. Depending on which one is at fault, and the type of fault, you may see text on the screen or you may see nothing at all. However, you will *hear* something and this is your clue as to what's going on.

The sound you hear will be a series of beeps, which are known as beep codes because they have a meaning. Each code is different and indicates a fault (usually non-specific) with one of the devices. Short of replacing each of them with one that is known to work (how many people have a spare motherboard lying around?), these codes are the only way of pin-pointing the offending device.

Before you can decipher the beep codes, you will need to know the manufacturer of the BIOS chip in your system. The reason for this is that it is the BIOS that produces the beep codes and different BIOS manufacturers use different codes. You will find this information in the PC's documentation. It may also be stamped on the top of the BIOS chip, which is located on the motherboard (see page 17).

The following tables show an abbreviated list of the most common beep codes (see margin note).

Hot tip

As far as the upgrader is concerned, problems with any of these devices will almost certainly be restricted to connection issues. The beep codes will tell you which device has a problem; just check the relevant connections.

Hot tip

A complete list of BIOS manufacturers' beep codes are available on the Internet.

- AMI beep codes can be found at www. ami.com

- Award beep codes can be found at www. phoenix.com

AMI BIOS	
Beeps	**Faulty Device**
1, 2 or 3	Memory (RAM). Reseat the module. If that doesn't work, replace it
4 to 7, 9 to 11	Motherboard or expansion card. Remove all the expansion cards; if the system still beeps, the motherboard is faulty. Otherwise, one of the expansion cards is faulty
8	Video System

...cont'd

AWARD BIOS	
Beeps	Faulty Device
1	This is normal and indicates that everything is OK
1 long, 2 short	Video system
Any other sequence	Memory

If the beep codes indicate a motherboard fault, remove all the expansion cards and reboot the PC. If it still refuses to start, then the motherboard or CPU (see margin note) is faulty. If the PC does start, however, one of the cards is faulty. Replace them one by one, rebooting each time until the faulty card is identified.

NOTE: if you have an AWARD BIOS and hear no beep codes at all, you almost certainly have a faulty motherboard. This will be confirmed by a dead keyboard (no lights). However, this does not apply to AMI BIOSs.

With regard memory modules, if you have just one installed, reseat it; the problem may be a bad connection. If this doesn't work, try moving it to a different slot (it is not unknown for a slot to develop a fault). If that doesn't work either, the module is faulty. However, if you have two, remove one and reboot. If there is still no joy, reinstall it, remove the other one and try again. While it's very unusual, it is possible for a faulty module to prevent the other one from working.

Moving on to video, if you are using a video card physically remove the card and then replace it to make sure the connection is good.

If the motherboard has an integrated video system, you can use this to check the video card. All you have to do is connect the monitor to the integrated system and boot the PC. If it starts, you have confirmed what the beep codes were telling you. However, if you are already using the integrated video system, you will have to either replace the motherboard or fit a video card.

NOTE: text on the boot screen indicates that the video system is OK (with no video, you have no text).

Hot tip

Reseating the CPU has been known to work; it's a long-shot but it might just do the trick.

Hot tip

If your PC has both an integrated video system and a video card, you can use one to check the other.

169

Hard Drive

Hard drive failure is easy to recognize; the system will usually get no further than the "Detecting hard drives" stage when it is started. You will see this on the first boot screen immediately after the memory test, as shown below.

Hot tip

Depending on the nature of the problem, you may get an error message as well.

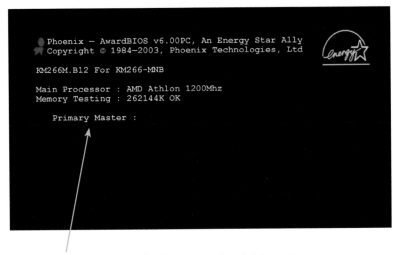

Phoenix — AwardBIOS v6.00PC, An Energy Star Ally
Copyright © 1984—2003, Phoenix Technologies, Ltd

KM266M.B12 For KM266-MNB

Main Processor : AMD Athlon 1200Mhz
Memory Testing : 262144K OK

    Primary Master :

Bootup stops at the Detecting hard drives stage

With recent systems, if the drive's model number is not listed on the bootup screen there is a problem with the drive itself, its power supply or its connections.

The first thing to check is that the drive is powered up. Open the case and connect a different power plug to the drive. This does two things: firstly, it establishes whether or not there is power at the plug and, secondly, ensures that the actual connection is good.

Next, make sure that the interface cable is securely socketed at both ends. If you happen to have a spare one, try using this. If there is still no joy, the drive is faulty.

With older systems, the problem could also be a configuration fault in the BIOS. Carry out the above checks and if they don't resolve the issue, the next thing to investigate is the drive's BIOS configuration. Do this as follows:

Hot tip

If the drive is listed on the boot screen, it has been recognized by the BIOS. This is a good sign that it is probably OK. This scenario is more likely on older systems and the problem will usually be a configuration issue.

1 Enter the BIOS Setup program and open the Standard CMOS Features page. Next to IDE Primary Master, you should see None (if everything was OK, the drive's model number would be listed here)

Hot tip

Users with an AMI BIOS should go to the Advanced Page and then the IDE Configuration page.

```
                 Phoenix - AwardBIOS CMOS Setup Utility
                        Standard CMOS Features
┌─────────────────────────────────────────────────┬─────────────────┐
│ Date (mm:dd:yy)         Fri, March 26 2006        │    Item Help    │
│ Time (hh:mm:ss)         14 : 1 : 19               │                 │
│                                                   ├─────────────────┤
│ IDE Primary Master      [None]                    │ Menu Level      │
│ IDE Primary Slave       [None]                    │                 │
│ IDE Secondary Master    [None]                    │ Press (enter)   │
│ IDE Secondary Slave     [None]                    │ to enter next   │
│                                                   │ page for detail │
│ Drive A                 [1.44MN 3.5]              │ of hard drive   │
│ Drive B                 [None]                    │ settings.       │
│                                                   │                 │
│ Video                   [EGA/VGA]                 │                 │
│ Halt On                 [All Errors]              │                 │
│                                                   │                 │
│ Base Memory             640K                      │                 │
│ Extended Memory         522346K                   │                 │
│ Total Memory            522346K                   │                 │
└─────────────────────────────────────────────────┴─────────────────┘
```

2 Select IDE Primary Master and press Enter. This will open the hard drive Auto-Detection page, as shown below

```
                 Phoenix - AwardBIOS CMOS Setup Utility
                        Standard CMOS Features
┌─────────────────────────────────────────────────┬─────────────────┐
│ IDE HDD Auto-Detection      [Press Enter]         │    Item Help    │
│                                                   │                 │
│ IDE Primary Master          [Auto]                ├─────────────────┤
│ Access Mode                 [Auto]                │ Menu Level      │
│                                                   │                 │
│                                                   │ To auto-detect  │
│ Capacity                    400022MB              │ the HDD's size, │
│                                                   │ head on this    │
│                                                   │ channel         │
│ Cylinder                                          │                 │
│ Head                                              │                 │
│ Precomp                                           │                 │
│ Landing Zone                                      │                 │
│ Sector                                            │                 │
└─────────────────────────────────────────────────┴─────────────────┘
```

3 Select IDE HDD Auto-Detection and press Enter

The BIOS will now attempt to configure the drive by loading its parameters.

If it succeeds, the drive's parameters will be displayed, as shown below. Save the changes, exit the BIOS and reboot the PC. The problem should now be resolved.

Modern BIOSs auto-detect the PC's drives every time it is started. With older BIOSs this is not the case; if a drive's configuration is lost, it will stay lost until the user reconfigures it manually.

172

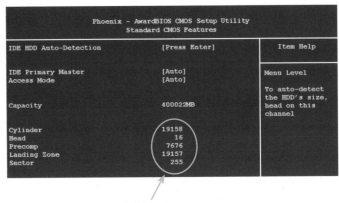

Hard drive parameters

If the BIOS cannot load the drive's parameters, the drive is faulty and will have to be replaced.

Another problem that can occur is the boot procedure stopping at the "Verifying DMI Pool Data" stage, as shown below.

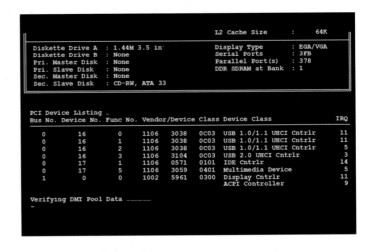

Hot tip

It is a fact that many PC problems can be "fixed" by simply switching off and then back on. This is always worth a try.

This is often caused by a transient configuration problem that can be resolved by switching off for a few seconds. If not, it will be a hard drive connection issue that will be fixed by reseating the drive's interface cable connections.

Video

Blank Display

Upgraders probably have more trouble with video cards than any other part of the system. One of the most common problems is installing a new video card and starting the PC only to see it stop with a blank screen at the point where Windows is beginning to load.

There are three likely causes of this and they all involve settings in the BIOS.

1) Some BIOSs have a setting which must be set according to the type of video card being used. The default setting is usually PCI, so if you install an AGP or PCI Express card, the setting must be altered accordingly

2) In some PCs that provide integrated video, it will be disabled automatically when a video card is installed. In others, however, it won't be and this can cause all sorts of problems. In this type of system there will be a BIOS setting that allows the user to manually disable the integrated video

3) There is a setting in the BIOS that allows the user to change the AGP Aperture Size (see top margin note) of an AGP video card. This will be set by the computer's manufacturer to a figure that's suitable for the installed AGP card. However, if the user decides to upgrade to a more recent AGP card, it might not work with the existing aperture setting. If this is the case, a blank screen may be the result. The solution, therefore, is to find a setting that will be compatible with the new card

Do this as follows:

1. Enter the BIOS Setup program

2. Select Advanced Chipset Features and press Enter

3. At the next screen, select AGP & P2P Bridge Control

Hot tip

In theory, the AGP Aperture Size should be set to half the amount of installed memory. In practice, however, this setting sometimes causes problems, in which case a different setting will have to be selected.

Hot tip

Users with an AMI BIOS should go to the Advanced page, Chipset Configuration and then AGP.

...cont'd

4 Select AGP Aperture Size

Hot tip

Finding the optimum
AGP aperture setting
is not of critical
importance. If your
display works at the 64M
setting, it's OK to leave it
at that.

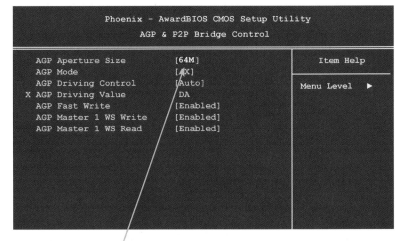

```
                 Phoenix - AwardBIOS CMOS Setup Utility
                      AGP & P2P Bridge Control

   AGP Aperture Size          [64M]              Item Help
   AGP Mode                    [ 4X]
   AGP Driving Control         [Auto]         Menu Level    ►
 X AGP Driving Value            DA
   AGP Fast Write              [Enabled]
   AGP Master 1 WS Write       [Enabled]
   AGP Master 1 WS Read        [Enabled]
```

5 Use the Page Up/Page Down keys to select the [64M]
option

Return to the main BIOS page, save the change and then exit the
BIOS. Reboot the PC and the display should now be restored.

However, finding the *optimum* AGP setting is a matter of
trial and error, so keep redoing the above procedure, selecting a
higher setting each time, until you find the highest one at which
Windows will load.

Resolution/Color Depth Cannot Be Changed

This is a common problem and is a result of the video card driver
having become corrupted or uninstalled. Check this out by going
to Start, Control Panel, Personalization, Display Settings. Click
the Advanced Settings tab and then click Adapter. If the driver
is present and correct, you will see the video system listed under
Adapter Type. If it is not, click Properties, the Driver tab, and
then Update Driver.

Scrambled Display

Another problem that can occur when a video card is installed, is
being greeted by a scrambled (an unintelligible mass of colored
lines) display when the PC is booted. This is usually caused by the
monitor's refresh rate being too high. Resolve it as follows:

Hot tip

A corrupted DirectX
driver can also be the
cause of a scrambled
display. Check this out
by installing the latest
version.

1 Reboot into Safe Mode (see page 165)

2 When back in Windows, go to Start, Control Panel, Personalization, Display Settings. Click the Advanced Settings tab and then click the Monitor tab

In Safe Mode, Windows will start the PC with a generic "no-frills" video driver that works with all setups.

3 Using the drop-down box, select a lower refresh rate

175

Flickering Display (Applies to Windows XP Only)

A flickering display is caused by a refresh rate that is set too low. Users of Windows XP may find that after installing a new video card (or Windows XP itself), Windows has chosen a very low (often the lowest possible) refresh rate. This results in noticeable screen flicker, which can be extremely irritating.

Resolve it as follows:

1) Right-click the Desktop, select Properties, Settings, Advanced

2) Click the Monitor tab and then select the highest available refresh rate (usually 85 Hertz). Click OK

Hot tip

If the refresh rate is too low, it will cause screen flicker, and if it is too high, it will scramble the display.

Sound

A new sound card has been installed but unfortunately it's not producing any.

One likely cause is that the PC's integrated sound system has not been disabled. Do this as follows:

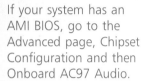

Hot tip

If your system has an AMI BIOS, go to the Advanced page, Chipset Configuration and then Onboard AC97 Audio.

1. Enter the BIOS Setup program and on the main page select Integrated Peripherals

2. Select the "xxx Onchip PCI Device" (xxx is the name of the chipset manufacturer, e.g. Via), and press Enter

3. Find the setting that relates to AC97 Audio and select Disabled

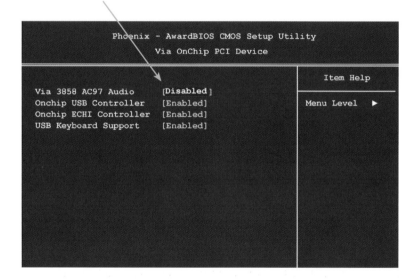

```
          Phoenix - AwardBIOS CMOS Setup Utility
                   Via OnChip PCI Device

                                                    Item Help

   Via 3858 AC97 Audio      [Disabled]
   Onchip USB Controller    [Enabled]      Menu Level    ▶
   Onchip ECHI Controller   [Enabled]
   USB Keyboard Support      [Enabled]
```

Hot tip

If you have just installed a new CD/DVD drive and aren't getting any sound from it, check that you have connected the drive's audio cable to the PC's sound system (see pages 101-102).

The next thing to check is that the speakers are connected to the sound card and not the integrated system – this is an easy mistake to make.

Then make sure that the speakers are connected to the right jack. This will be stamped as Line Out, Speaker Out or Audio Out.

Check that the speakers are powered up and that volume controls, both on the speakers and in Windows, are turned up.

If there's still no sound, check the sound driver as described on the next page. Finally, check the card's motherboard connection.

In a situation where the sound has been working and then suddenly stopped, suspect the sound system's driver immediately.

1 Go to Start, Control Panel, Sound. Then click the Audio tab

2 If there is nothing listed under the Playback and Recording tabs then the driver is either corrupted or hasn't been installed

3 Reinstall the driver to restore the sound

If the driver is OK (indicated by the boxes being active), the problem is hardware related. Check the speakers and their connections as per the previous page.

If the sound is still not working, in the case of an integrated system, the motherboard will need to be replaced. A more practical solution, however, would be to simply buy a sound card.

In the case of a sound card, connect the speakers to the PC's integrated system (after enabling it in the BIOS). If it works now, there is a problem with the sound card. Check that it is securely connected to the motherboard; failing that it will have to be replaced.

Beware

Sound system drivers are notorious for corruption. If your PC suddenly loses its sound, this is the first thing to check.

Don't forget

System Restore is an ideal way of quickly resolving a sound system driver issue.

Modems

Dial-Up Modems

If the modem won't dial out, check the following:

Is it installed? – check that it is listed under the Modem category in Device Manager. If it isn't, reinstall the driver from the installation disk. If it still won't dial, you need to dig deeper.

Modem Diagnostic Check – open Device Manager in the Control Panel, locate the modem and right-click it. Select Properties. In the dialog box which opens, click the Diagnostics tab and then click "Query Modem".

1. If you see a list of "AT" commands, this indicates that the modem is working and that the problem is software related

2. Go back to the Control Panel and click Network and Sharing Center. Click manage Network Connections on the left-hand side and then right-click the modem connection. Then click Delete

3. Now reinstall the connection. If this was created with a CD from your ISP, then insert the disk and follow the instructions. Alternatively, you can use Windows New Connection Wizard

If the modem dials out now, then its software configuration was corrupt.

If, however, the AT commands don't appear in the diagnostic test, or you see a "Port Already In Use" message, then the modem is probably using the wrong COM port. Check the modem's documentation to see which port it is designed to use. Then open Device Manager, right-click the modem and select Properties. Click the Advanced tab and then Advanced Port Settings. Check that the modem is set to the right port as per the documentation.

If there is still no joy, the modem is faulty.

Broadband Modems

You've just installed a modem, hooked it up to your broadband connection, switched on, fired-up your browser and .... nothing. All you get is "This page cannot be displayed".

Check the following:

LEDs – all broadband modems have a number of LEDs, each of which indicate something specific. Unfortunately, no two modems are the same in this respect so we can't help you on this – you'll need to consult the documentation.

Look for the LED that indicates whether or not the modem is receiving data. If it is lit, this tells you that the ISP's servers are OK, and that the incoming connection to the modem is as well. If it is not, either your ISP's servers are down (contact them to verify this) or there is a bad connection between the cable input to the house and the modem.

Then check the LED that indicates a good connection between the modem and the PC. If this is out, make sure the cable is plugged in securely at both ends. If you are using a USB modem, check that USB is enabled in the BIOS (see page 63).

Modem driver – open Device Manager and make sure that the modem is listed under Network Adapters. If not, reinstall its driver. If there is a warning symbol next to the modem, double-click it to see what the problem is.

Software – reinstall the ISP's software from the installation disk. If there is still no joy, you should find a diagnostic utility on the installation disk; most ISPs supply one. These utilities can resolve software configuration issues.

As a last resort, you'll have to contact the ISP's technical support.

Monitors

Faults with these devices are very rare but when they do occur, will be either a total failure or some sort of image distortion. Fortunately, particularly in the case of expensive monitors, they can be repaired and there are many repair shops available for this purpose.

Note that CRT monitors carry potentially lethal voltages, and so the average user should never open one up. Troubleshooting, therefore, is restricted to establishing conclusively that the device is faulty – once done, take it to a specialist.

With regard to image problems, you don't need a degree to figure this one out. Troubleshooting a blank display isn't too difficult either. The first thing to check (as with all electrical or electronic equipment) is the power supply; if the front panel LED is lit, the device has power, if it isn't, it doesn't have power. In the latter case, check that there is power at the wall socket and that the power cord (including the fuse in the plug) is sound, and firmly connected.

If the LED is lit, the monitor is either in standby mode, in which case pressing the on/off button once will bring it to life, or it is in power management mode. Pressing a key or clicking the mouse should return it to normal operation.

Note that in some systems, the power management mode may be reluctant to relinquish its grip and a considerable amount of key bashing or mouse clicking may be necessary.

If the screen is still blank, switch off both the PC and the monitor, and then disconnect the VGA or DVI cable from the video system. Switch the monitor back on and if you now see a test signal, as shown opposite, the monitor is OK; the problem will be with the PC's video system. Otherwise, you have a faulty monitor.

Inkjet Printers

If your printer refuses to print anything, your first move should be to switch it off and then back on. Doing so can resolve many configuration issues. If this doesn't work, do the same thing with the PC.

Next, establish whether the fault lies with the printer itself or with the system. This is done with the aid of the printer's test page facility; all printers have one of these.

The procedure varies from printer to printer, so you will have to consult the documentation. Typically, though, it involves isolating the device from the PC by disconnecting the interface cable, powering it up and then pressing a combination of buttons. If the printer is OK, it prints a page full of random characters. You then know that the problem is either a connection issue or is software related.

In this case, the first thing to check is that the interface cable is securely connected. If you are using an old parallel port printer that is linked to the PC via another device, such as a Zip drive, bypass the device and connect the printer directly (any problems with the other device may interfere with the printer).

Then make sure the printer is correctly installed. Do this by opening Printers and Faxes (Printers if you are running Windows Vista) in the Control Panel; if the device is installed it will be listed here. If it isn't, dig out the driver disk and reinstall it. While you have this window open, make sure that you don't have two or more copies of the driver installed. If you do, delete all of them and then reinstall it.

If you have more than one printer installed, make sure that the one malfunctioning isn't set as the default printer (click the device and from the Printer menu, deselect "Set as default printer" if it is).

Finally, check the application that you are printing from, as it is possible for a corrupt program to refuse to communicate with the printer. Type a few lines into Notepad and see if it prints.

If the test page doesn't print, check that the ink cartridges actually contain ink. Then run the head cleaning utility to make sure that the ink nozzles aren't simply blocked with dried ink. This is quite likely if the printer hasn't been used for a while.

Hot tip

A common cause of problems with printers is transient configuration faults. These can be resolved by the simple expedient of switching off for a few seconds.

Hot tip

Blocked print head nozzles are a common cause of print failure and this is usually caused by lack of use.

Scanners

Problems with scanners, particularly newly installed scanners, are usually related to incorrect connections and power issues.

Parallel Port Scanners

For those of you who may still be using an old parallel port scanner, there are two likely problems with these devices:

1) Connecting the scanner to the PC via the "Out" socket. These scanners have two parallel port sockets at the back (as shown below) – one for incoming data and one for outgoing data. You must use the "In" socket

2) Connecting the scanner to the PC via another parallel port device such as a Zip drive or printer. Any problems with the other device will prevent the scanner from working as well

USB Powered Scanners

USB scanners usually draw their power from the USB interface, and as USB can provide only a limited amount, it may be that the scanner is drawing more than the interface can provide. This will only happen when you have other USB powered devices connected to the system.

The temporary solution is to simply disconnect as many of the other devices as necessary. For a permanent fix, you will need to buy an AC powered USB hub (shown left) that will supply all the power your USB devices need.

Initialization Failure

This is a common problem with scanners and will announce itself with a "Scanner Initialization Failed", or similar, error message. There are several causes of this: the scanner hasn't been connected to the system, it isn't powered up or you have selected the wrong driver in the scanning program.

If none of these are causing the problem, however, leave the scanner switched on and reboot the PC. On restart, very often, the scanner will suddenly be operational.

Hot tip

A common problem with some scanners is initialization failure. If you get an error message to this effect, try rebooting the computer while the scanner is switched on. This action initializes the scanner's internal settings, and on restart, it will usually work.

CD/DVD Drives

Usually, when these devices have a physical problem, the relevant drive icon will be missing in My Computer.

Reboot the PC, and on the first boot screen you should see the drive listed next to Secondary Master. If it isn't, the drive is either faulty or has a connection problem (if it's a newly installed drive, it will be the latter). Open the system case and check that the power and interface cables are securely connected. If the interface cable is an older 40-pin cable, try reversing the connection to the drive (it is possible to connect them the wrong way round). If the system still doesn't recognize the drive, it is faulty.

If the drive is listed on the boot screen but not in My Computer then it has a configuration problem (see margin note). See if the drive is listed in Device Manager and whether any problems are reported there. If so, try the suggested remedy. Failing that, do the following:

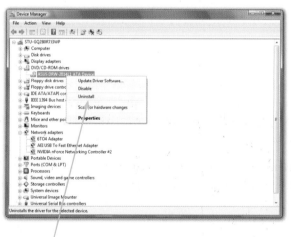

1   Right-click the drive and click Uninstall

2   Switch the computer off and physically disconnect the drive by removing both the power and interface cables. Then reconnect them and reboot. Windows will see the device as a new addition to the system and automatically assign it a new channel, which should resolve the issue

If the drive isn't listed in Device Manager, follow the procedure described in Step 2 above.

Windows

We could write a book about troubleshooting Windows but with just two pages available here, we'll have to restrict ourselves to the biggest fault of all – refusal to start.

Windows XP

When XP has a fault serious enough to prevent it from starting (note what we are saying here – faults with XP itself, not other applications preventing it from running), the boot procedure will come to a halt with an error message. There are quite a few of these but the two most common are:

- System32\config\system File is Missing or Corrupt

- NTLDR is Missing

Either of these error messages indicate that XP's startup files are corrupt, so no matter how many times you reboot, the result will be the same. The solution lies in the form of the boot disk we showed you how to make on page 166. Slip it into the floppy drive, reboot and, hey presto, XP will start as normal.

A more serious fault is when XP itself is seriously corrupted. When this happens, bootup stops with a "Disk Boot Failure" error message, as shown below.

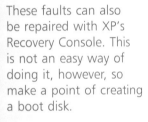

Hot tip

These faults can also be repaired with XP's Recovery Console. This is not an easy way of doing it, however, so make a point of creating a boot disk.

184

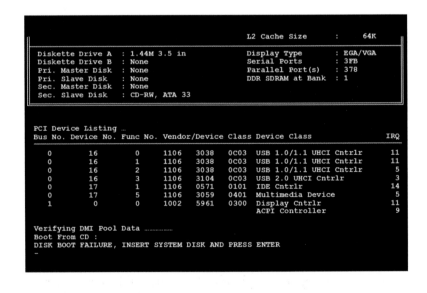

This error message indicates that the BIOS has been unable to locate the operating system. There are two possible causes for this. The first, as we've already mentioned, is that XP is corrupted and the second is a faulty hard drive (where the operating system lives).

The hard drive is the first thing to look at (see pages 170-172). If it checks out OK, the problem is with XP and it will need repairing.

Dig out XP's installation disk and make sure the system is set to boot from the CD-ROM drive (see page 88). Put the disk in the drive and reboot. When you see the message saying "Press any key to boot from CD", do so.

Hot tip

If the XP installation is damaged beyond repair, you will have to reinstall XP. This is the type of situation where a data backup, as described on page 12 will be a life-saver.

```
Windows XP Home Edition Setup

  Welcome to Setup.

  This portion of the Setup program prepares Microsoft(R)
  Windows(R) XP to run on your computer.

    • To set up Windows XP now, press ENTER.

    • To repair a Windows XP installation using
      Recovery Console, press R.

    • To quit Setup without installing Windows XP, press F3.
```

1 At the first screen, select Set up Windows XP by pressing Enter. At the second, select the Repair Windows XP option and press R

```
Windows XP Home Edition Setup

  If one of the following Windows XP installations is damaged,
  Setup can try to repair it.

  Use the UP and DOWN ARROW keys to select an installation.

    • To repair the selected Windows XP installation,
      press R.
    • To continue installing a fresh copy of Windows XP
      without repairing, press ESC.

    C:\WINDOWS "Microsoft Windows XP Home Edition"
```

Hot tip

Viruses can also be the cause of operating system corruption.

185

The XP installation will now be repaired. However, if you don't see an operating system (highlighted in white), this means that XP has been corrupted beyond repair. Your only option in this case will be to do a new installation.

Windows Vista

Vista offers users more options with which to repair a faulty installation. As with XP, the PC must be set to boot from the CD/DVD drive as explained on page 88.

Then boot the PC from the installation disk and when you see the message "Press any key to boot from CD...", do so.

1. At the first screen, click Next and at the following screen, click Repair your computer

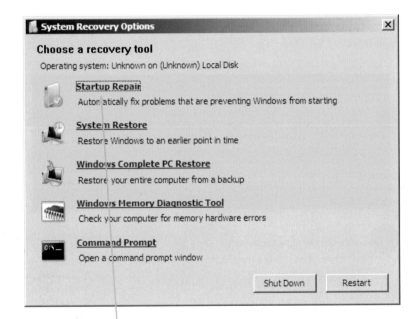

2. Click Startup Repair at the System Recovery Options screen

Vista will now check it's startup files, which are the most likely cause of the problem, and if they are damaged it will replace them from the installation disk. The PC will then automatically reboot and all should now be well.

If the PC still refuses to boot up however, then the Vista installation is damaged beyond repair and you will need to reinstall it.

Index

W